THE GUITAR STRUMMERS'
ROCK
SONGBOOK

ISBN 978-1-4234-9433-1

HAL•LEONARD®
CORPORATION
7777 W. BLUEMOUND RD. P.O. BOX 13819 MILWAUKEE, WI 53213

For all works contained herein:
Unauthorized copying, arranging, adapting, recording, Internet posting, public performance,
or other distribution of the printed music in this publication is an infringement of copyright.
Infringers are liable under the law.

Visit Hal Leonard Online at
www.halleonard.com

CONTENTS

STRUM IT GUITAR LEGEND

Strum It is the series designed especially to get you playing (and singing!) along with your favorite songs. The idea is simple – the songs are arranged using their original keys in lead sheet format, providing you with the authentic chords for each song, beginning to end. Rhythm slashes are written above the staff. Strum the chords in the rhythm indicated. Use the chord diagrams found at the top of the first page of the arrangement for the appropriate chord voicings. The melody and lyrics are also shown to help you keep your spot and sing along.

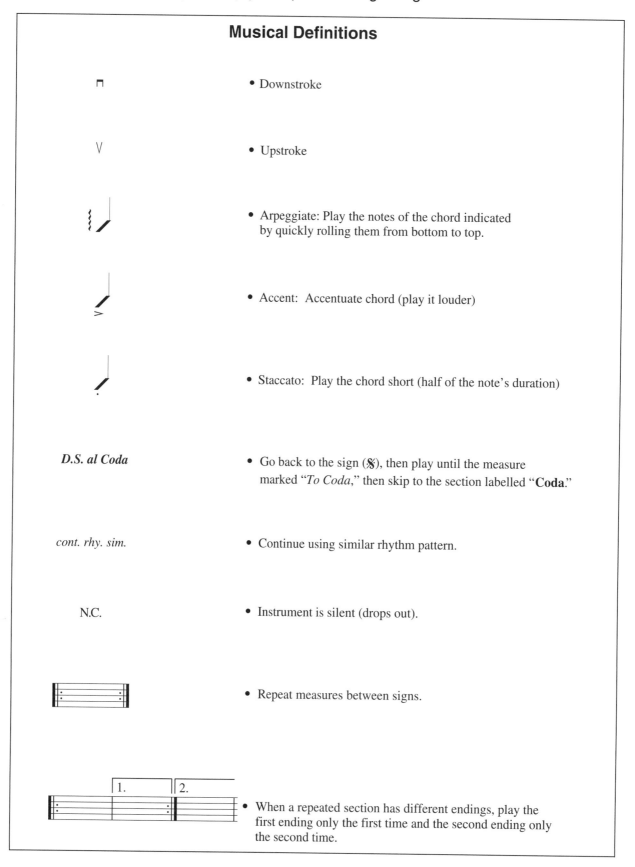

Musical Definitions

- Downstroke

- Upstroke

- Arpeggiate: Play the notes of the chord indicated by quickly rolling them from bottom to top.

- Accent: Accentuate chord (play it louder)

- Staccato: Play the chord short (half of the note's duration)

D.S. al Coda
- Go back to the sign (𝄋), then play until the measure marked "*To Coda*," then skip to the section labelled "**Coda**."

cont. rhy. sim.
- Continue using similar rhythm pattern.

N.C.
- Instrument is silent (drops out).

- Repeat measures between signs.

1.   2.
- When a repeated section has different endings, play the first ending only the first time and the second ending only the second time.

Against the Wind

Words and Music by Bob Seger

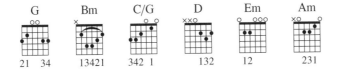

Intro
Moderately

1. I seems like yes - ter - day, ___ but it was ___ long a - go. _____
2. And the years rolled ___ slow-ly past, and I found my - self a - lone. ___
3. *Piano solo*

Ja - ney was love - ly, she was the queen of my nights _____
Sur-round - ed by strang - ers I thought were my friends, _____

there ___ in the dark - ness with the ra - di - o playing low. ___ And
I found my - self fur - ther and fur - ther from my home. And I

Copyright © 1980 Gear Publishing Co.
All Rights Reserved Used by Permission

G

and the se-crets that we _ shared,
guess I lost my way

Bm

the moun - tains that we moved. _
there were oh, so man-y roads. _

C/G

Caught like a wild - fire _ out of _ con - trol _
I was liv - ing to run _ and run-ning to live, _

G

till there was
nev - er wor -

C/G

noth-ing left to burn _ and noth-ing left to prove. _
- ied a - bout pay - ing or e - ven how much I owed.

D

1. And I re -
2. Mov - ing eight _
3. Well, those

Pre-Chorus

Em

mem - ber _ what she _ said to me, _
_ miles a min - ute _ for months at a time, _
drift - er's days _ are _ past me now.

D

G

how she swore _
break - ing all _
I've got so _

Em
cont. rhy. sim.

_ that it nev - er would end.
_ of the rules _ that would bend.
_ much more to think a - bout.

C/G

G

Em

I re - mem-ber how she held _ me, oh, _
I be - gan to find my - self search -
Dead-lines and com -

D

Chorus

1. A - gainst the wind, ___ we were run - nin' a - gainst ___ the
2. A - gainst the wind, ___ lit - tle some-thing a - gainst ___ the
3. A - gainst the wind, ___ I'm still run - nin' a - gainst ___ the

wind. ___ We were young ___ and strong, we were run - nin' a - gainst ___ the
wind. ___ I found ___ my - self ___ seek - ing shel - ter a - gainst ___ the
wind. ___ I'm old - er now ___ but still run - nin' a - gainst ___ the

wind. ___
wind. ___
wind. ___

3.

Well, I'm old - er now ___ and still run - nin' a - gainst the

Outro
w/ Lead Voc. ad lib. on repeat

Repeat and fade

wind. A - gainst the wind. A - gainst the

American Pie

Words and Music by Don McLean

Copyright © 1971, 1972 BENNY BIRD CO., INC.
Copyright Renewed
All Rights Controlled and Administered by SONGS OF UNIVERSAL, INC.
All Rights Reserved   Used by Permission

9

mu-sic save your ___ mor-tal soul? An' ___ can you teach me ___ how to dance ___ real ___

___ slow? _____ Well, I ___ know that you're ___ in love with him, ___'cause I ___

___ saw you danc-in' in the gym. ___ You both kicked off ___ your shoes. _____ Man, I

dig those rhy-thm-ic blues. _____ I was a lone-ly teen-age ___

bronc-in' buck ___ with a pink car-na - tion an' a pick-up ___ truck. ___ But

I knew I ___ was out _____ of luck, the day ___ the mu - sic died. ___

___ I start-ed sing-in', ___ "Bye, ___ He was sing-in', ___ "Bye, ___

this -'ll be the day _ that I ___ die." They were sing - in',

Outro-Chorus
Moderately fst

"Bye, _____ bye, Miss A - mer - i - can Pie. ___ Drove my Chev - y to the lev - ee but the

cont. rhy. sim.

lev - ee was dry. ___ Them good ol' ___ boys ___ were drink - in' whis - key an' rye, ___ sing - in',

this - 'll be the day ___ that I ____ die." _____

Additional Lyrics

2. Now for ten years we've been on our own, and moss grows fat on a rollin' stone.
   But, that's not how it used to be.
   When the jester sang for the king and queen in a coat he borrowed from James Dean,
   And a voice that came from you and me.
   Oh, and while the king was looking down, the jester stole his thorny crown.
   The courtroom was adjourned; no verdict was returned.
   And while Lenin read a book on Marx, the quartet practiced in the park,
   And we sang dirges in the dark the day the music died.
   We were singin',...

3. Helter-skelter in a summer swelter, the birds flew off with a fallout shelter,
   Eight miles high and fallin' fast.
   It landed foul on the grass. The players tried for a forward pass,
   With the jester on the sidelines in a cast.
   Now the half-time air was sweet perfume, while the sergeants played a marching tune.
   We all got up to dance, oh, but we never got the chance
   'Cause the players tried to take the field; the marching band refused to yield.
   Do you recall what was revealed the day the music died?
   We started singin',...

4. Oh, and there we were all in one place, a generation lost in space,
   With no time left to start again.
   So come on, Jack be nimble, Jack be quick! Jack flash sat on a candlestick,
   'Cause fire is the devil's only friend.
   Oh, and as I watched him on the stage, my hands were clenched in fists of rage.
   No angel born in hell could break that Satan's spell.
   And as the flames climbed high into the night to light the sacrificial rite,
   I saw Satan laughing with delight the day the music died.
   He was singin',...

Can't Buy Me Love

Words and Music by John Lennon and Paul McCartney

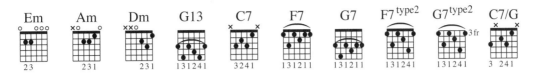

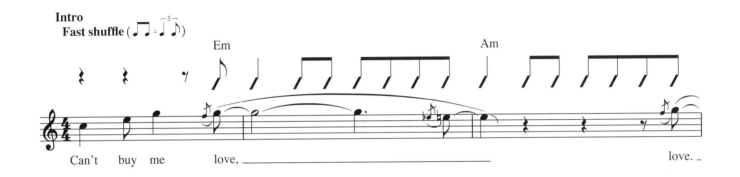

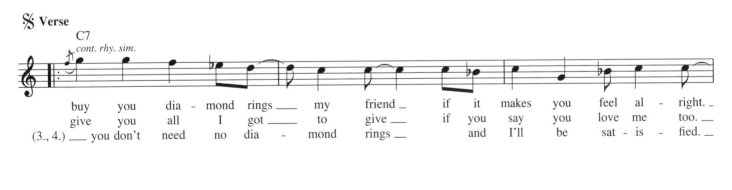

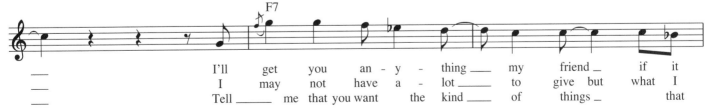

Copyright © 1964 Sony/ATV Music Publishing LLC
Copyright Renewed
All Rights Administered by Sony/ATV Music Publishing LLC, 8 Music Square West, Nashville, TN 37203
International Copyright Secured   All Rights Reserved

makes you feel al - right. ____
got I'll give to you. ____
mon - ey just can't buy. ____

'Cause I don't care too

To Coda ⊕ | 1.

much for mon - ey, mon - ey can't buy me love. ____ 2. I'll

| 2.

Bridge

____ Can't buy me love, _____ ev -

cont. rhy. sim.

- 'ry - bod - y tells me so. Can't buy me love, _____ uh,

| 3.

no, no, no, ____ no. _____ 3. Say ____ Ow! _____

Guitar Solo

Angie

Words and Music by Mick Jagger and Keith Richards

© 1973 (Renewed 2001) EMI MUSIC PUBLISHING LTD.
All Rights for the U.S. and Canada Controlled and Administered by COLGEMS - EMI MUSIC INC.
All Rights Reserved   International Copyright Secured   Used by Permission

Additional Lyrics

2. Angie, you're beautiful,
But ain't it time we said goodbye?
Angie, I still love you.
Remember all those nights we cried?
All the dreams we held so close
Seemed to all go up in smoke.
Let me whisper in your ear:
"Angie, Angie,
Where will it lead us from here?"

Baby Hold On

Words and Music by Eddie Money and James Douglas Lyon

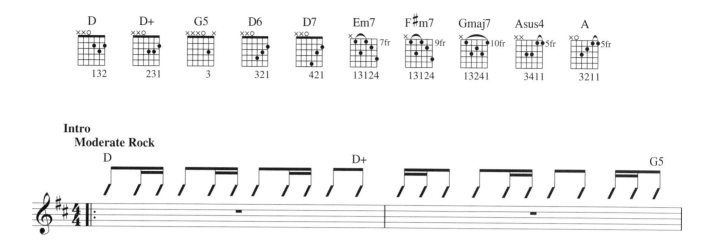

Intro
Moderate Rock

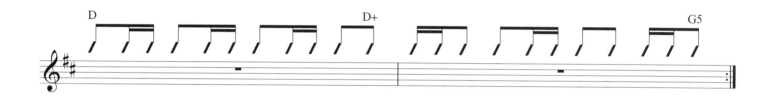

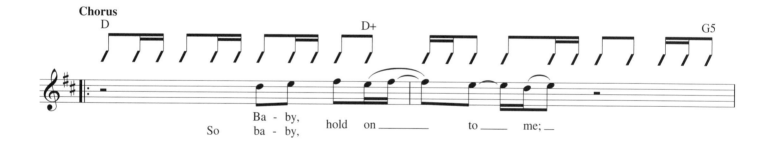

So ba-by, Ba-by, hold on _____ to _____ me; _____

what-ev-er will be. _____ will _____ be _____ 'Cause the, the, The fu-ture is ours _____

_____ to _____ see, _____ so ba-by, when you hold on _____ to _____ me. _ 1. Ba-

Copyright © 1977 (Renewed) by Three Wise Boys Music LLC (BMI)
International Copyright Secured   All Rights Reserved

Verse

- by, what's _ these things you been say - in' a - bout _____ me be - hind my _____ back? _
2. *See additional lyrics*

_____ Is it true you might want a bet - ter life? _ Is it

true you think this is things I like, _____ uh?

Pre-Chorus

Think a - bout it, ba - by;
See additional lyrics

I'm _____ gon - na take you to the top. _____

Chorus

So ba - by, hold on _____ to _____ me; _

cont. rhy. sim.
what - ev - er will be _____ will be. _ The fu - ture is ours _____

_____ to _____ see _____   when you hold on _____ to _____ me, _____ whoa. _____

Pre-Chorus

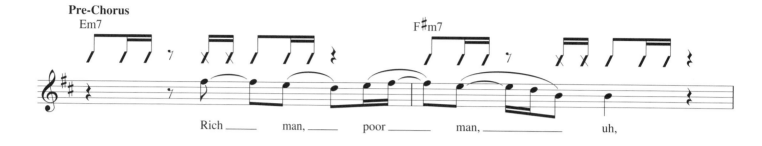

Rich _____ man, _____ poor _____ man, _____ uh,

real - ly don't mean all _____ that much. _____

Ma - ma's al - ways told _____ you, girl, _____ that

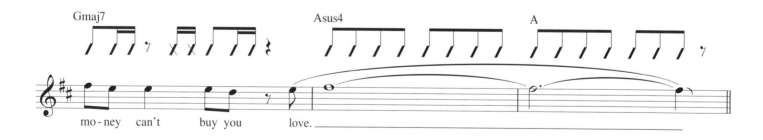

mo - ney can't buy you love. _____

𝄉 Chorus

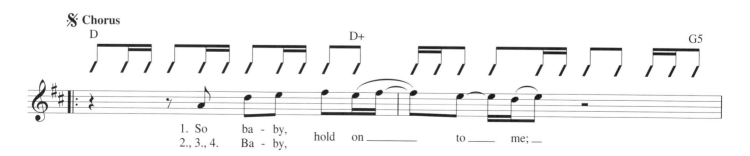

1. So ba - by,   hold on _____ to _____ me; _____
2., 3., 4. Ba - by,

Additional Lyrics

2. Hey, baby, you know the future's lookin' brighter
Every mornin' when I get up.
Don't be thinkin' 'bout what's not enough now, baby,
Just be thinkin' 'bout what we got.

Pre-Chorus Think of all my lovin', now.
I'm gonna give you all I got.

Baby, I Love Your Way

Words and Music by Peter Frampton

Copyright © 1975 ALMO MUSIC CORP. and NUAGES ARTISTS MUSIC LTD.
Copyright Renewed
All Rights Controlled and Administered by ALMO MUSIC CORP.
All Rights Reserved   Used by Permission

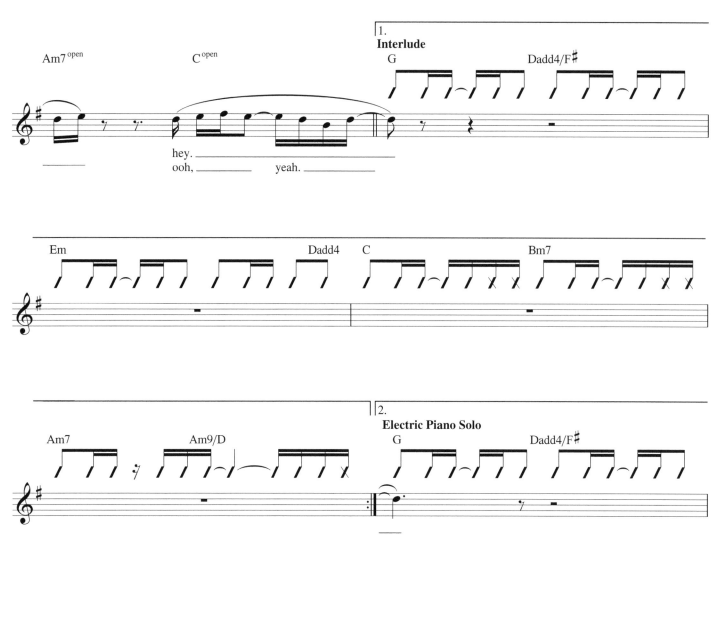

Am7 open   C open

1. Interlude
G   Dadd4/F♯

hey. _____
ooh, _____ yeah. _____

Em   Dadd4 C   Bm7

Am7   Am9/D

2. Electric Piano Solo
G   Dadd4/F♯

Em   Dadd4 C   F9

G   Dadd4/F♯   Em   Dadd4   C   F9
cont. rhy. sim.

But

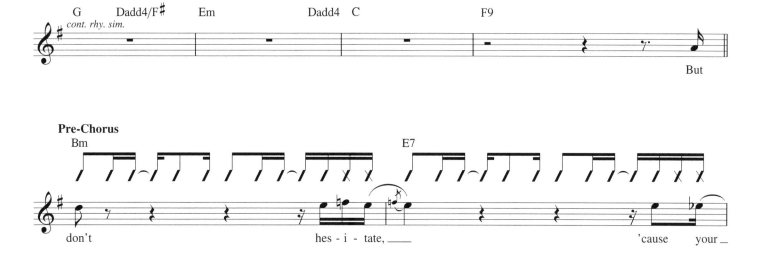

Pre-Chorus
Bm   E7

don't   hes - i - tate, _____   'cause your _

24

Band on the Run

Words and Music by Paul McCartney and Linda McCartney

© 1974 (Renewed) PAUL and LINDA McCARTNEY
Administered by MPL COMMUNICATIONS, INC.
All Rights Reserved

Verse

2. If I ev-er get out __ of here, thought of giv-ing it all __ a-way __ to a reg-is-tered char-i-ty. __ All I need is a pint __ a day. __ If I ev-er get out __ of here. __ (If we ev-er get out __ of here.) __

Interlude

3. Well, the

Verse

rain ex-plod-ed with a might-y crash __ as we fell in-to ____ the sun.
un-der-tak-er drew a heav-y sigh __ see-ing no one else __ had come.
night was fall-ing as the des-ert world _ be-gan to set-tle down.

And the first one said to the sec-ond one there __ I
And a bell was ring-ing in the vil-lage square __ for the
In the town they're search-ing for us ev-'ry-where __ but we

cont. rhy. sim.

Best of My Love

Words and Music by John David Souther, Don Henley and Glenn Frey

Cmaj7add2 C Fmaj7#11 Fmaj7 Cmaj7 Fmaj7b5 F

Em7 Dm7 G G7 G6 Fm

Intro
Moderately slow

Cmaj7add2 / C   Cmaj7add2 / C   Fmaj7#11 / Fmaj7   Fmaj7#11 / Fmaj7

% Verse

Cmaj7 / C   Cmaj7 / C   Fmaj7b5 / Fmaj7   Fmaj7b5 / Fmaj7

1. Ev-er-y night ___ I'm ly-in' in bed ___ hold-in' you close ___ in my dreams; ___
2., 3. *See additional lyrics*

Cmaj7 / C
cont. rhy sim.
F

think-in' a-bout ___ all the things that we ___ said and com-in' a-part ___ at the seams. ___

Em7   Dm7   Em7   F

We tried to talk it o - ver ___ but the words come out ___ too ___ rough. I

Cmaj7 / C   Fmaj7   Cmaj7 C   **To Coda** ⊕   G G7 G6 G7

1.

know you were try - in' to give me the best ___ of your ___ love.

2.
G
Chorus
C
F

(Whoa, _____ sweet dar - lin'.)
You get the best of my ___ love, you get the best of my ___

© 1974 (Renewed 2002) EMI BLACKWOOD MUSIC INC., CASS COUNTRY MUSIC and RED CLOUD MUSIC
All Rights Reserved   International Copyright Secured   Used by Permission

Additional Lyrics

2. Beautiful faces an' loud empty places, look at the way we live;
   Wastin' our time on cheap talk and wine, left us so little to give.
   That same old crowd was like a cold dark cloud that we could never rise above.
   But here in my heart I give you the best of my love.

3. But ev'ry morning I wake up and worry what's gonna happen today.
   You see it your way and I see it mine but we both see it slippin' away.
   You know we always had each other, baby, I guess that wasn't enough;
   Oh, oh, but here in my heart I give you the best of my love.

Blaze of Glory

Words and Music by Jon Bon Jovi

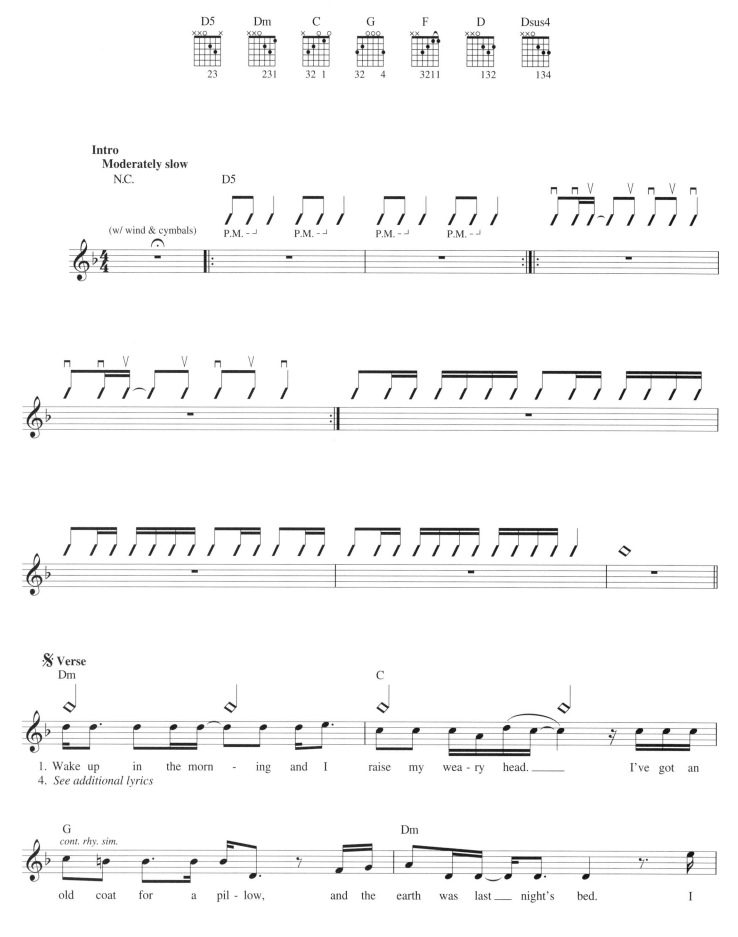

Copyright © 1990 UNIVERSAL - POLYGRAM INTERNATIONAL PUBLISHING, INC. and BON JOVI PUBLISHING
All Rights Controlled and Administered by UNIVERSAL - POLYGRAM INTERNATIONAL PUBLISHING, INC.
All Rights Reserved   Used by Permission

don't know where I'm go - ing. On - ly God knows where I've been. I'm a

To Coda 1 ⊕

dev - il on the run, a six - gun lov - er, a can - dle in the wind. Yeah!

D5

Verse
Dm

2. When you're brought in - to this world, they
3. *See additional lyrics*

C .... G

cont. rhy. sim.

say you're born in sin. Well, at least they gave me some - thing. I did - n't have to

Dm .... F

steal, or have to win. Well, they tell me that I'm want - ed, yeah.

C .... G

I'm a want - ed man. I'm a colt in your sta - ble. I'm what Cain was to A - ble, mis - ter,

Additional Lyrics

3. You ask about my conscience, and I offer you my soul.
   You ask if I'll grow to be a wise man, well I ask if I'll grow old.
   You ask me if I've known love, and what it's like to sing songs in the rain.
   Well, I've seen love come, I've seen it shot down, I've seen it die in vain.

4. Each night I go to bed, I pray the Lord my soul to keep.
   No, I ain't looking for forgiveness, but before I'm six feet deep,
   Lord, I got to ask a favor, and I hope you'll understand,
   'Cause I've lived life to the fullest, let this boy die like a man.
   Staring down a bullet, let me make my final stand.

Come Monday

Words and Music by Jimmy Buffett

Copyright © 1974 SONGS OF UNIVERSAL, INC.
Copyright Renewed
All Rights Reserved Used by Permission

side.

Bridge

And I can't ___ help ___ it, hon-ey, you're that much a part ___

___ of me now. ___ Re - mem-ber that night ___ in Mon - tan - a when we

Interlude

said there'd be no room ___ for doubt.

Coda

D.S. al Coda

side. I spent

four lone-ly days in a brown ___ L. A. haze, ___ and I just want you back by my

side. ___

Additional Lyrics

2. Yes, it's been quite a summer,
Rent-a-cars and west-bound trains.
And now, you're off on vacation,
Somethin' you've tried to explain.
And, darlin', it's "I love you so."
That's the reason I just let you go.

3. I hope you're enjoyin' the scen'ry;
I know that it's pretty up there.
We can go hikin' on Tuesday,
With you, I'd walk anywhere.
California has worn me quite thin;
I just can't wait to see you again.

Crazy Little Thing Called Love

Words and Music by Freddie Mercury

© 1979 QUEEN MUSIC LTD.
All Rights for the U.S. and Canada Controlled and Administered by BEECHWOOD MUSIC CORP.
All Rights for the world excluding the U.S. and Canada Controlled and Administered by EMI MUSIC PUBLISHING LTD.
All Rights Reserved   International Copyright Secured   Used by Permission

There goes my ba - by, ___ she knows how to rock 'n' roll. ___ She drives me cra - zy. ___

She gives me hot and cold fe - ver; she leaves me in a cool, cool sweat.

D.S. al Coda 1

3. I've got - ta be cool, ___

Coda 1

Guitar Solo

Dreams

Words and Music by Stevie Nicks

1. Now here you go a - gain, you say you want your free -
2. Now here I go a - gain, I see the crys - tal vi -

- dom. Well, who am I to keep you down?
- sion. I keep my vi - sions to my - self.

It's on - ly right that you should play the way you feel it. But
It's on - ly me who wants to wrap a - round your dreams. And

Copyright © 1977 Welsh Witch Music
Copyright Renewed
All Rights Administered by Sony/ATV Music Publishing LLC,
8 Music Square West, Nashville, TN 37203
International Copyright Secured   All Rights Reserved

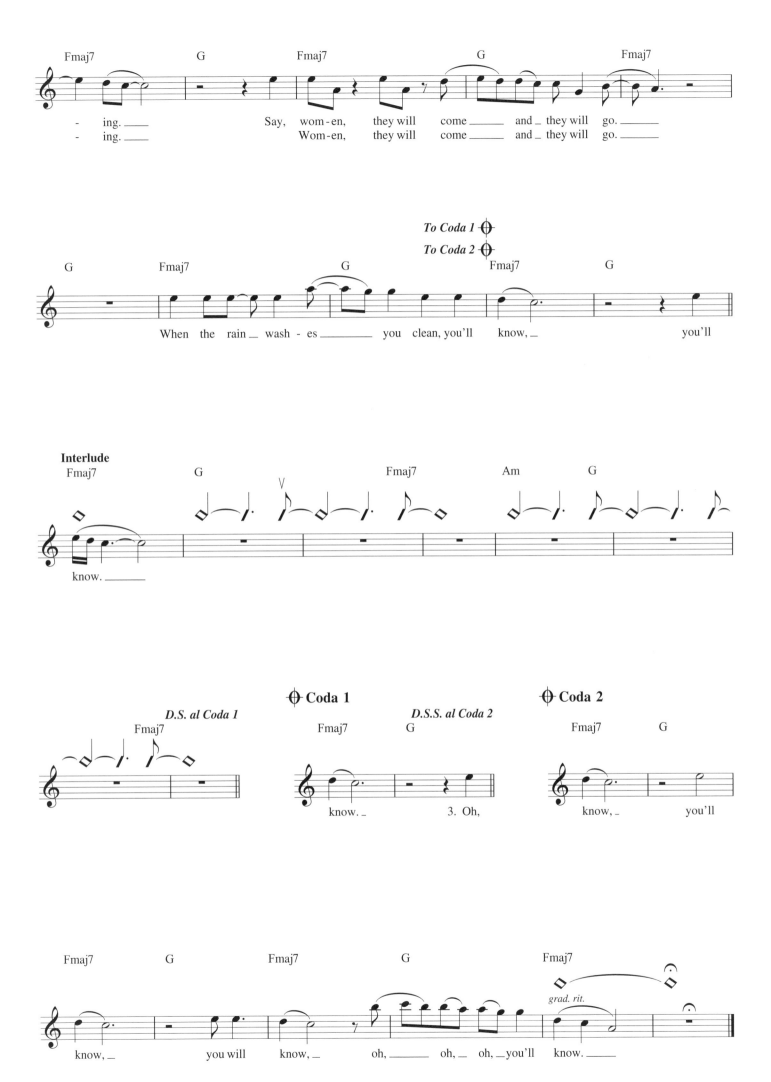

Day After Day

Written by Peter Ham

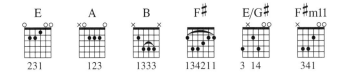

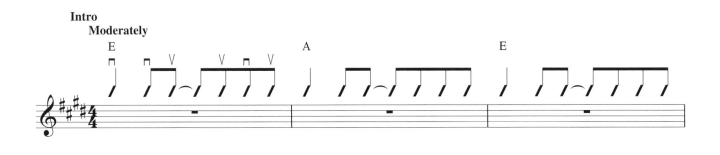

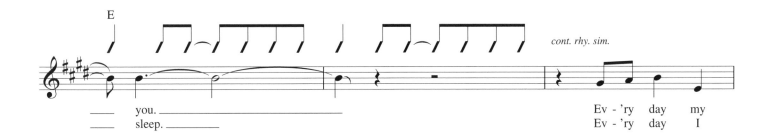

© 1971 (Renewed 1999) BUG MUSIC INC. (BMI) o/b/o BUG MUSIC LTD. (PRS)
All Rights Reserved   Used by Permission

Daydream

Words and Music by John Sebastian

Copyright © 1966 by Alley Music Corp. and Bug Music-Trio Music Company
Copyright Renewed
International Copyright Secured All Rights Reserved
Used by Permission

Additional Lyrics

4. What a day for a daydream,
   Custom made for a daydreaming boy.
   And I'm lost in a daydream,
   Dreamin' 'bout my bundle of joy.

Drift Away

Words and Music by Mentor Williams

Copyright © 1972 ALMO MUSIC CORP.
Copyright Renewed
All Rights Reserved   Used by Permission

Chorus

give me the beat,_ boys, and free my soul._ I wan-na get lost in your rock and roll _ and

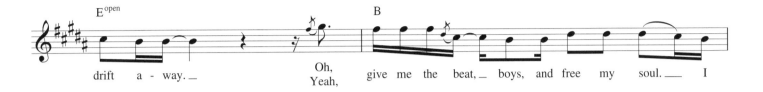

drift a - way. _ Oh, Yeah, give me the beat,_ boys, and free my soul. _ I

wan - na get lost in your rock and roll __ and drift a - way. _

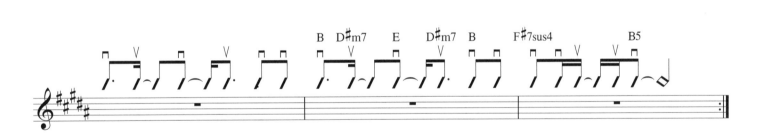

Bridge

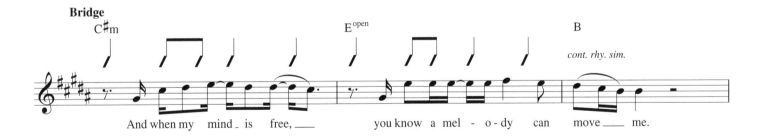

And when my mind _ is free, ___ you know a mel - o - dy can move ___ me.

D.S. al Coda

And when I'm feel - in' blue, _ the guit-ar's com-in' through _ to soothe _ me. ___

Fooling Yourself
(The Angry Young Man)

Words and Music by Tommy Shaw

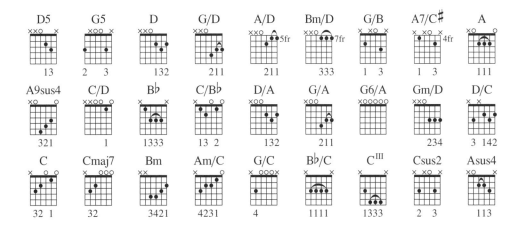

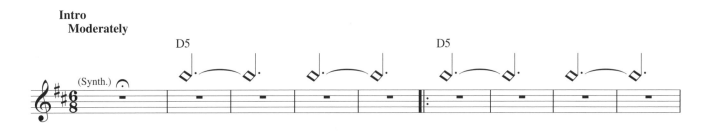

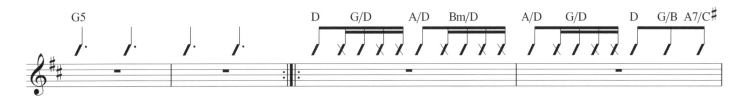

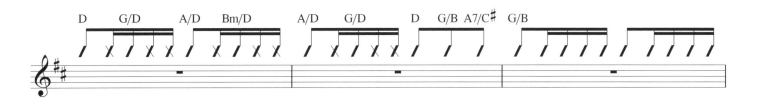

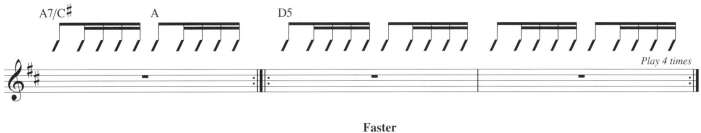

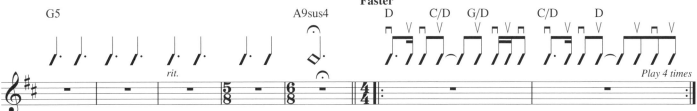

Copyright © 1977 ALMO MUSIC CORP. and STYGIAN SONGS
Copyright Renewed
All Rights Controlled and Administered by ALMO MUSIC CORP.
All Rights Reserved   Used by Permission

Verse

1. You see the world through your cyn-i-cal eyes. You're a trou-bled young man I can
2. *See additional lyrics*

tell. You got it all in the palm of your hand, but your

hand's wet with sweat, and your head needs a rest. And you're

Chorus

fool - ing your - self if you don't be - lieve it. You're

1. kid - ding your - self if you don't be - lieve it.

2. kill - ing your - self if you don't be - lieve it. Get up!

Bridge

(Get up!) Get back on your feet. You're the one they can't beat and you

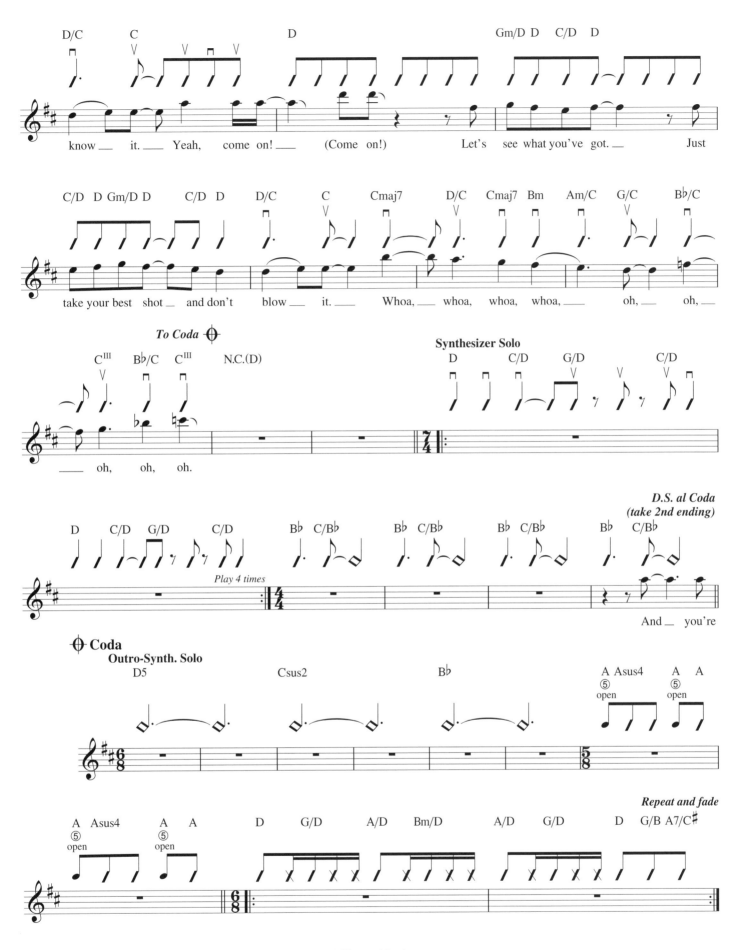

Additional Lyrics

2. Why must you be such an angry young man
When your future looks quite bright to me?
And how can there be such a sinister plan
That could hide such a lamb,
Such a caring young man?

Evil Ways

Words and Music by Sonny Henry

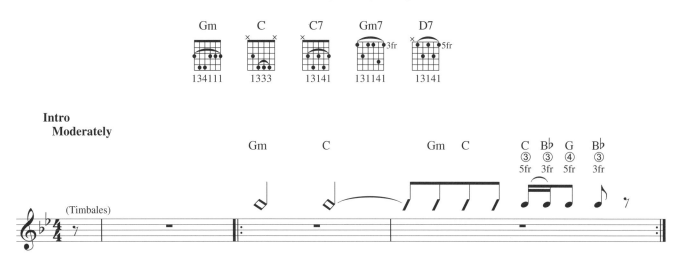

Intro
Moderately

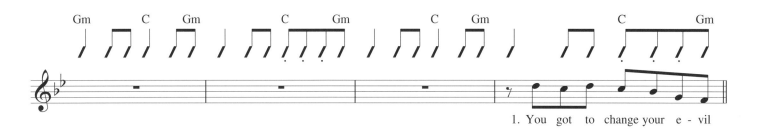

1. You got to change your e - vil

ways,   ba - by,   be - fore   I   start   lov-in'   you. _ You got to
(2., 3.) home, _   ba - by,   my house is dark and my   pots are   cold. _ You hang-in'

change, _   ba - by,   and ev-'ry word _ that I   say   is true. You got me
'round, _   ba - by,   with Jean and Joan _ and a, who knows who. I'm get-tin'

run - nin'   and hid - in'   all _ o - ver town. _ You got me sneak-in'   and a peep - in'   and
tired _ of wait-in'   and fool-ing a - round. _ I'll find some-bod - y   that won't make me

Copyright © 1967 UNIVERSAL - SONGS OF POLYGRAM INTERNATIONAL, INC.
and RICHCAR MUSIC CORP.
Copyright Renewed
All Rights Controlled and Administered by
UNIVERSAL - SONGS OF POLYGRAM INTERNATIONAL, INC.
All Rights Reserved   Used by Permission

Feelin' Alright

Words and Music by Dave Mason

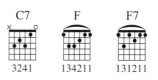

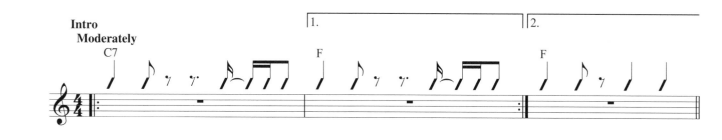

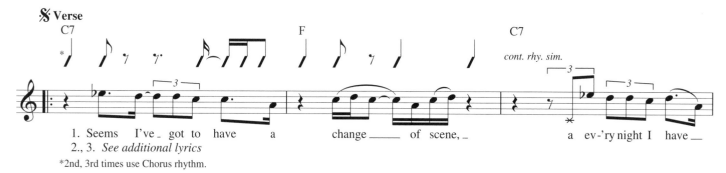

1. Seems I've got to have a change of scene, a ev'ry night I have
2., 3. *See additional lyrics*

*2nd, 3rd times use Chorus rhythm.

the strang-est dream. Im-pris-oned by the way it could have been.

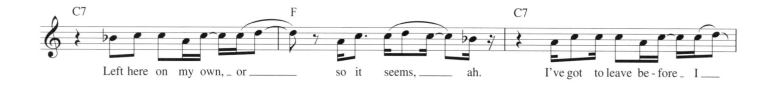

Left here on my own, or so it seems, ah. I've got to leave be-fore I

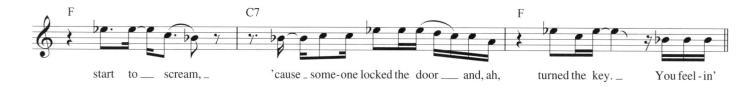

start to scream, 'cause some-one locked the door and, ah, turned the key. You feel-in'

Copyright © 1968, 1969 UNIVERSAL/ISLAND MUSIC LTD.
Copyrights Renewed
All Rights for the U.S. and Canada Controlled and Administered by
UNIVERSAL - POLYGRAM INTERNATIONAL PUBLISHING, INC.
All Rights Reserved Used by Permission

Additional Lyrics

2. Well, boy, you sure took me for one big ride,
And even now I sit and I wonder why.
Mm, a then a when I think of you I start myself to cry.
I just can't waste my time. I must keep dry.
Gotta stop believin' in all your lies,
'Cause there's too much to do before I die, hey!

3. Don't you get too lost in all I say.
Yeah, but at the time, you know I really felt that way.
But that was then and now you know it's today.
I can't get straight, so I guess I'm here to stay
Till someone comes along and takes my place, yeah,
With a diff'rent name, whoa, and a diff'rent face

The First Cut Is the Deepest

Words and Music by Cat Stevens

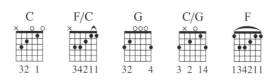

Copyright © 1967 SALAFA LTD.
Copyright Renewed
All Rights in the U.S. and Canada Controlled and Administered by UNIVERSAL MUSIC CORP.
All Rights Reserved   Used by Permission

Additional Lyrics

2., 3. I still want you by my side,
Just to help me dry the tears that I've cried.
{And / But} I'm sure gonna give you a try,
{And / 'Cause} if you want, I'll try to love again.
Baby, I'll try to love again, but I know...

Free Bird

Words and Music by Allen Collins and Ronnie Van Zant

Intro
Slow Rock

1. If I ___ leave ___ here to - mor - row, _____ would you ___ still re - mem - ber me?
2. *See additional lyrics*

Well, I must ___ be ___ trav - el - ing on ___ now, ___

'cause there's too man - y plac - es I've ___ got to see. ___

But if I ___ stay ___ here with ___ you, ___ girl, ___ things just could - n't be the same. ___

Copyright © 1973, 1975 SONGS OF UNIVERSAL, INC.
Copyright Renewed
All Rights Reserved   Used by Permission

Additional Lyrics

2. Bye bye, baby, it's been sweet now, yeah, yeah.
   Though this feelin' I can't change.
   A-please don't take it so badly,
   'Cause the Lord knows I'm to blame.
   But if I stay here with you, girl,
   Things just couldn't be the same.
   'Cause I'm as free as a bird now,
   And this bird you cannot change.
   Oh, and a bird you cannot change.
   And this bird you cannot change.
   Lord knows, I can't change.
   Lord help me, I can't change.

Give a Little Bit

Words and Music by Rick Davies and Roger Hodgson

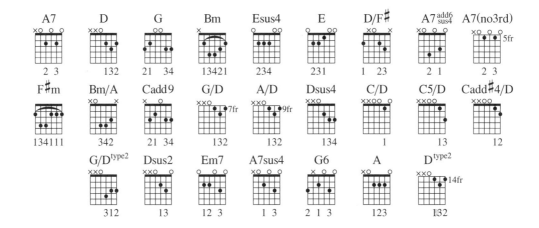

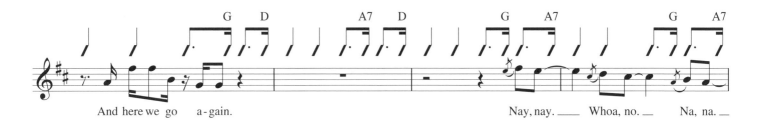

Copyright © 1977 ALMO MUSIC CORP. and DELICATE MUSIC
Copyright Renewed
All Rights Controlled and Administered by ALMO MUSIC CORP.
All Rights Reserved   Used by Permission

Into the Great Wide Open

Words and Music by Tom Petty and Jeff Lynne

Copyright © 1991 Gone Gator Music and EMI April Music Inc.
All Rights Reserved   Used by Permission

Chorus

In - to the great __ wide o - pen, under them skies __ of blue. Out in the great __ wide o - pen, a reb - el with - out __ a clue.

Interlude

D.S. al Coda

Coda

Outro-Chorus

In - to the great __ wide o - pen, un - der them skies __ of blue.

{ Out in / In - to } the great __ wide o - pen, a reb - el with - out __ a clue. __

Hey!

Additional Lyrics

2. The papers said Ed always played from the heart.
He got an agent and a roadie named Bart.
They made a record and it went in the charts.
The sky was the limit.
His leather jacket had chains that would jingle.
They both met movie stars, partied and mingled.
Their A and R man said, "I don't hear a single."
The future was wide open.

Jet Airliner

Words and Music by Paul Pena

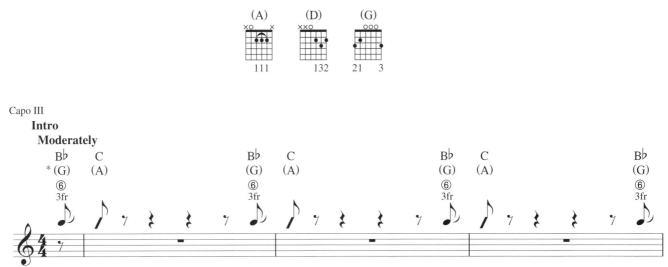

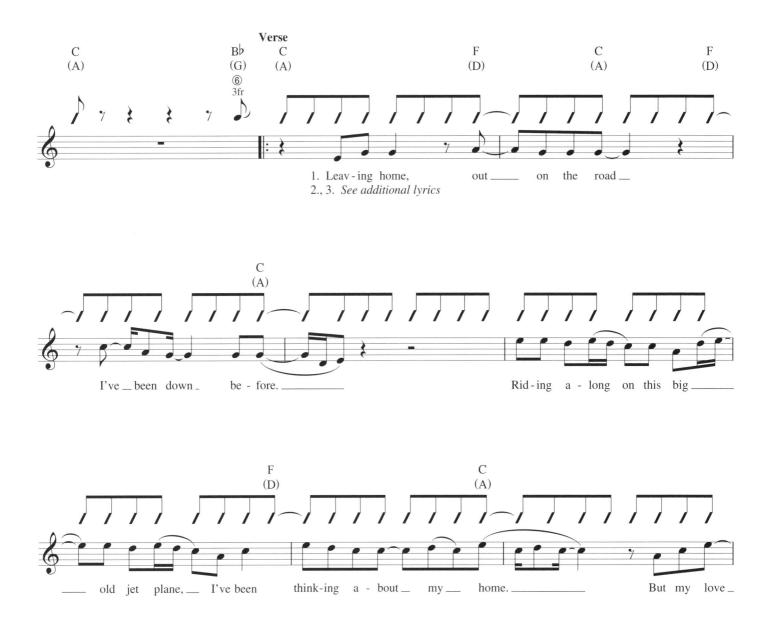

*Symbols in parentheses represent chord names respective to capoed guitar. Symbols above reflect actual sounding chords.

1. Leav-ing home, out on the road
2., 3. *See additional lyrics*

I've been down be-fore. Rid-ing a-long on this big old jet plane, I've been think-ing a-bout my home. But my love

Copyright © 1977 by Sailor Music and No Thought Music
Copyright Renewed
All Rights Administered by Sailor Music
All Rights Reserved Used by Permission

light seems so far a - way, and I feel like it's all been done.

Some-bod-y's try'n' to make me stay. You know I've

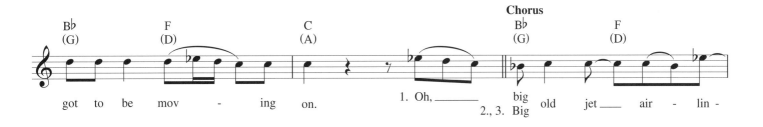
got to be mov - ing on. 1. Oh, big old jet air - lin -

2., 3. Big

Chorus

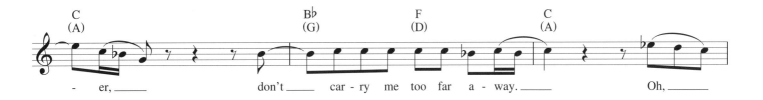
- er, don't car - ry me too far a - way. Oh,

big old jet air - lin - er, 'cause it's here that I've got to stay.

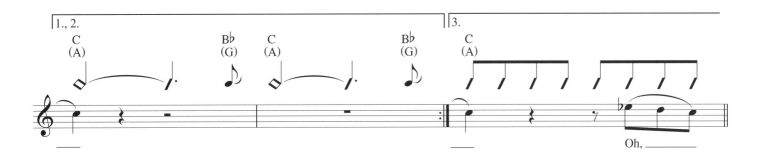
1., 2.

3.

Oh,

Additional Lyrics

2. Goodbye to all my friends at home.
   Goodbye to people I've trusted.
   I've got to go out and make my way.
   I might get rich, you know I might get busted.
   But my heart keeps calling me backwards
   As I get on the 707.
   Riding, high, I got tears in my eyes.
   You know you've got to go through hell before you get to heaven.

3. Touching down in New England town,
   Feel the heat coming down.
   I've got to keep on keeping on.
   You know the big wheel keeps a spinning around.
   And I'm going with some hesitation.
   You know that I can surely see
   That I don't want to get caught up
   In any of that funky kicks going down in the city.

Like the Way I Do

Words and Music by Melissa Etheridge

Copyright © 1988 ALMO MUSIC CORP. and M.L.E. MUSIC, INC.
All Rights Controlled and Administered by ALMO MUSIC CORP.
All Rights Reserved   Used by Permission

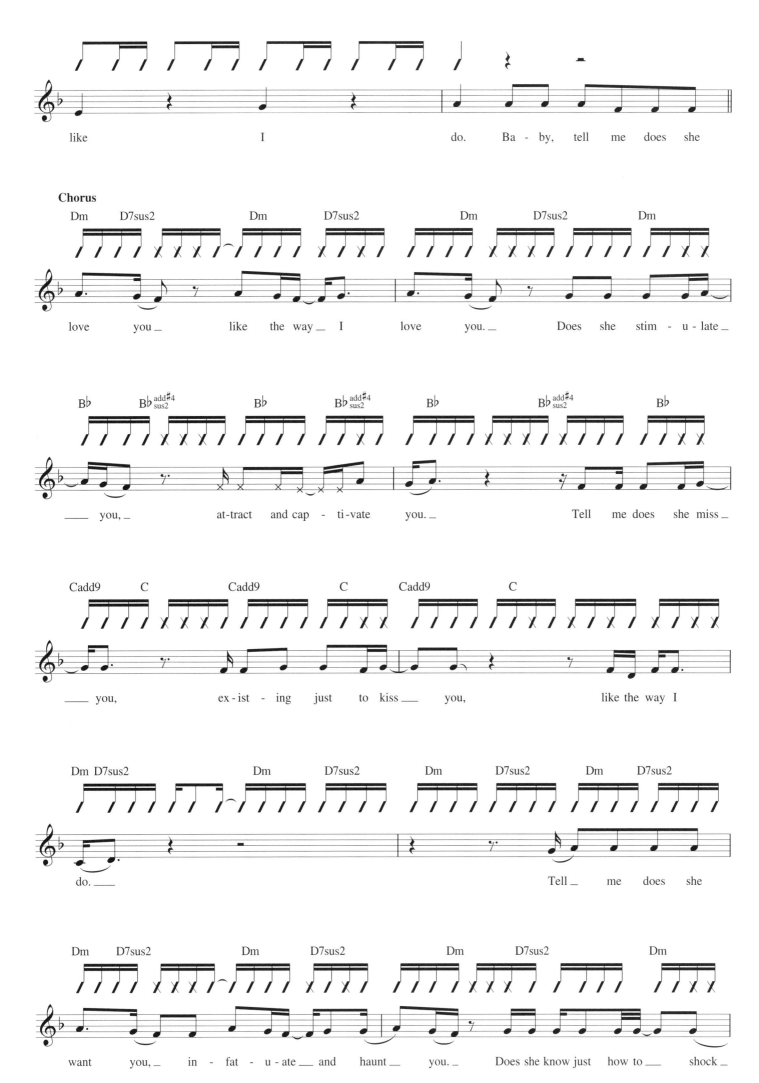

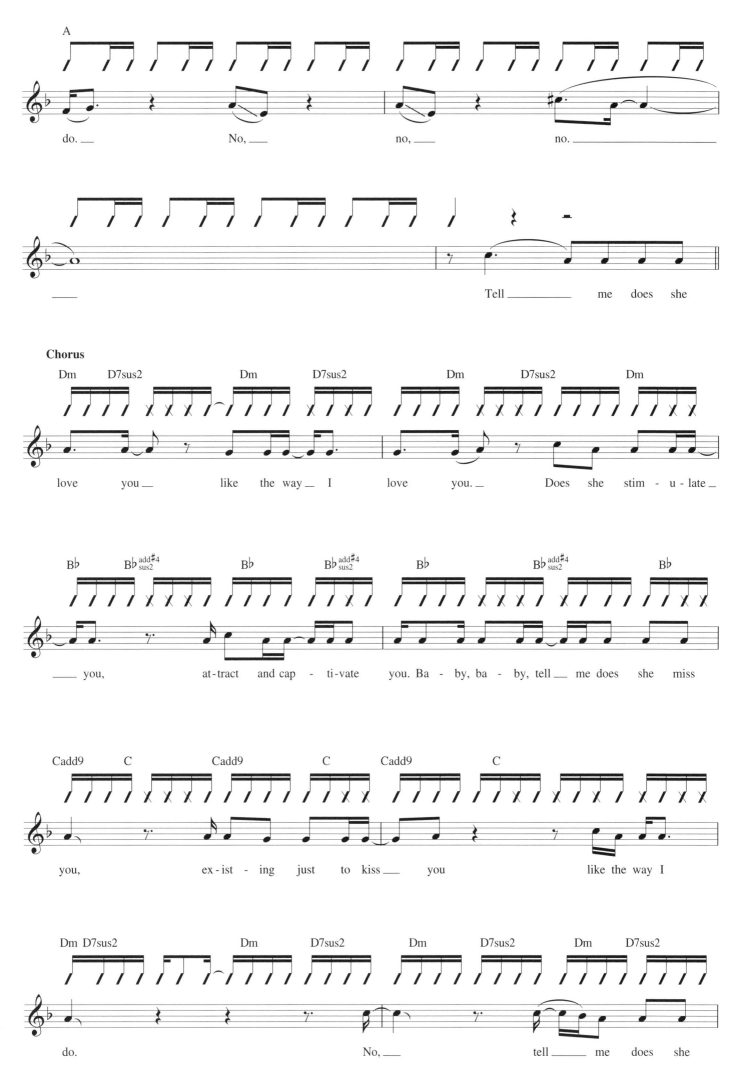

Additional Lyrics

2. Can I survive all the implications?
   Even if I tried could you be less than an addiction?
   Don't you think I know there's so many others
   Who would beg, steal and lie and fight, kill, and die,
   Just to hold you, hold you, like I do?

Learning to Fly

Words and Music by Tom Petty and Jeff Lynne

Copyright © 1991 Gone Gator Music and EMI April Music Inc.
All Rights Reserved   Used by Permission

Additional Lyrics

3. Well, some say life
Will beat you down,
And break your heart,
Steal your crown.
So I've started out
For God knows where.
I guess I'll know
When I get there.

Chorus I'm learning to fly
Around the clouds.
What goes up
Must come down.

Lodi

Words and Music by John Fogerty

Copyright © 1969 Jondora Music
Copyright Renewed
International Copyright Secured All Rights Reserved

stuck in a Lo - di a - gain. _____   2. A

Interlude

3. The

Coda

Interlude

Verse

cont. rhy. sim.

Mm. _____   4. If _____ I on - ly had a dol - lar for

ev -'ry song _ I sung, _____   ev -'ry time _ I've had to play _ while

*Bass plays B.   **Bass plays G.

peo - ple sat _ there drunk. _   You know I'd catch the next _____ train _____

***Bass plays B.   †Bass plays G.

back _ to where _ I live. _   Oh, Lord.   (I'm) stuck in a Lo - di a -

Outro

- gain. _____

Repeat & fade

Maggie May

Words and Music by Rod Stewart and Martin Quittenton

Copyright © 1971 by Unichappell Music Inc., Rod Stewart and EMI Full Keel Music Co.
Copyright Renewed 1999
All Rights for Rod Stewart Controlled and Administered by EMI Blackwood Music Inc.
International Copyright Secured   All Rights Reserved

but that don't wor-ry me none, in my eyes you're

ev - 'ry - thing. ___ I laughed at all of your jokes, ___ my

love you did-n't need to coax. ___ Oh, Mag-gie, I could-n't have

tried ___ an - y more. ___ 3., 4. You ___ 5. You made a

⊕ Coda
Guitar Solo

Outro

Repeat and fade

Additional Lyrics

3. You lured me away from home, just to save you from being alone.
   You stole my soul and that's a pain I can do without.
   All I needed was a friend to lend a guiding hand.
   But you turned into a lover and mother,
   What a lover, you wore me out.
   All you did was wreck my bed, and in the morning kick me in the head.
   Oh Maggie, I couldn't have tried any more.

4. You lured me away from home,
   'Cause you didn't want to be alone.
   You stole my heart; I couldn't leave you if I tried.
   I suppose I could collect my books and go on back to school.
   Or steal my daddy's cue and make a living out of playin' pool.
   Or find myself a rock 'n' roll band that needs a helping hand.
   Oh Maggie, I couldn't have tried any more.

5. You made a first-class fool out of me.
   I'm blind as a fool can be.
   You stole my heart, but I love you anyway.

Me and Bobby McGee

Words and Music by Kris Kristofferson and Fred Foster

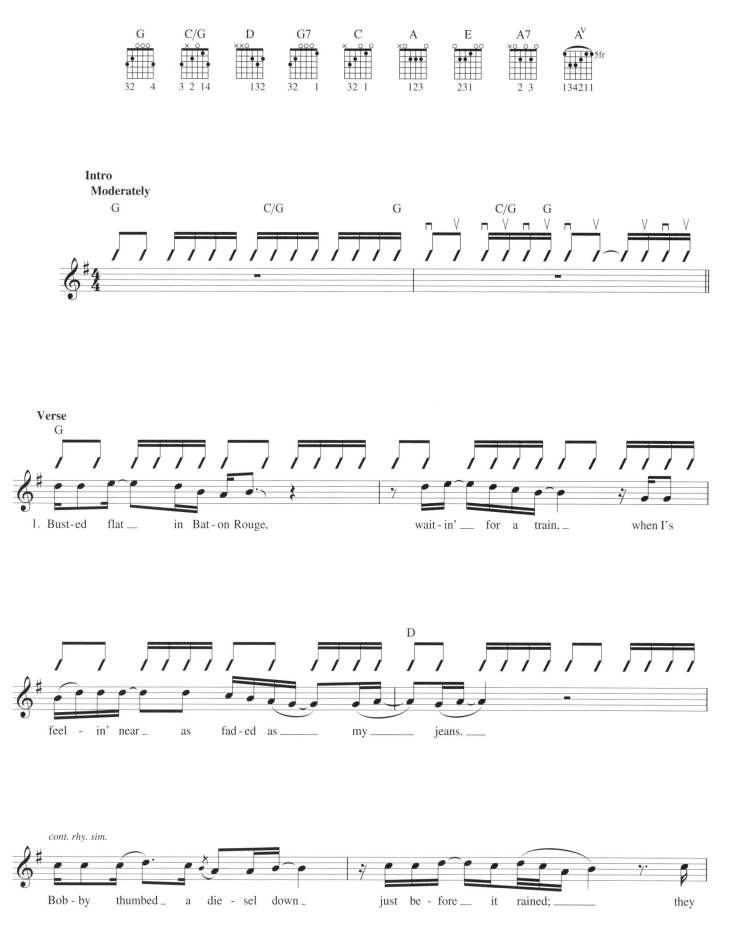

© 1969 (Renewed 1997) TEMI COMBINE INC.
All Rights Controlled by COMBINE MUSIC CORP. and Administered by EMI BLACKWOOD MUSIC INC.
All Rights Reserved   International Copyright Secured   Used by Permission

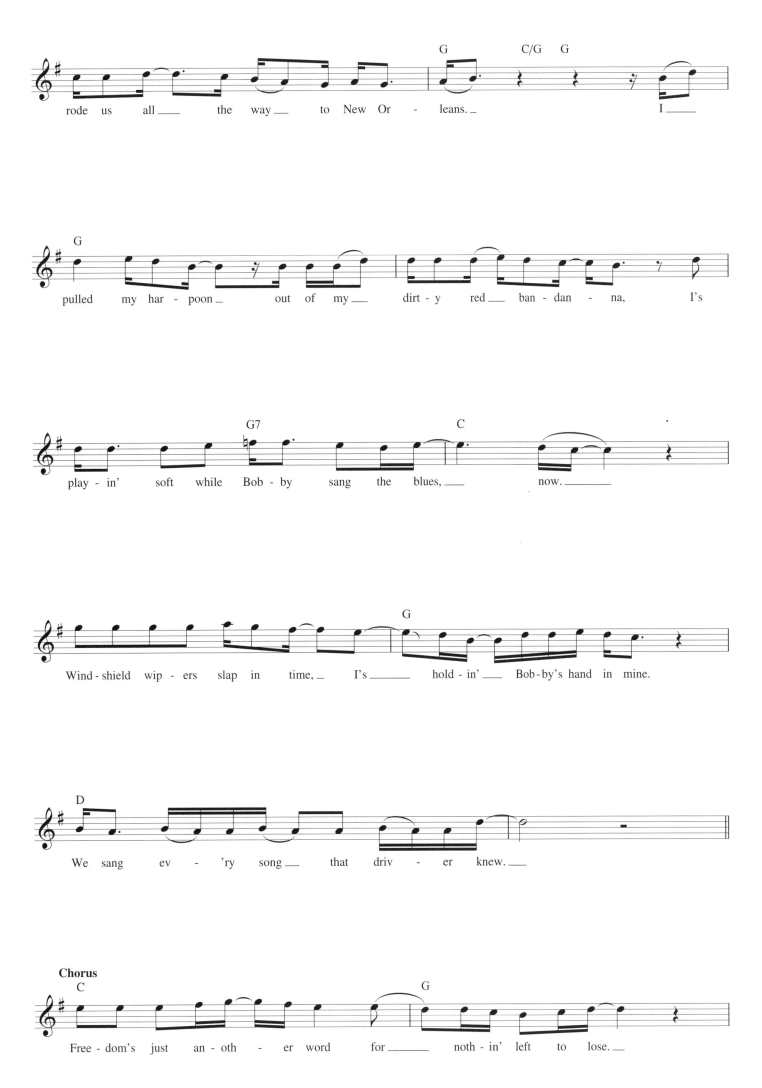

rode us all ___ the way ___ to New Or - leans. ___ I ___

pulled my har - poon ___ out of my ___ dirt - y red ___ ban - dan - na, I's

play - in' soft while Bob - by sang the blues, ___ now. ___

Wind - shield wip - ers slap in time, ___ I's ___ hold - in' ___ Bob - by's hand in mine.

We sang ev - 'ry song ___ that driv - er knew. ___

Chorus

Free - dom's just an - oth - er word for ___ noth - in' left to lose. ___

Noth - in', don't mean noth - in', hon', if it ain't free. _____ If

feel - in' good was eas - y, Lord, _____ when he sang the blues, _____ you know

feel - in' good was good e - nough _ for me, ___ good e - nough _ for me and my Bob - by Mc-

Verse

Gee. 2. From the Ken - tuck - y coal _ mines _ to the

Cal - i - for - nia sun, _ hey, Bob - by shared _ the se - crets of ___ my _____

_____ soul. Through all ___ kinds of weath - er, through ev - 'ry - thing _ we've done, _ yeah,

Bob - by, ba - by, helped me from the whole _ world. _ One day up near Sal - i - nas, Lord, _

good e-nough for me and my Bob - by Mc - Gee. 1. La, la,

Outro-Solo

la, la, la, la, la. La la, la, la, la, la, la.

2., 3. *See additional lyrics*
4., 5. *Piano solo*
6. *Guitar solo*

La, la, la, la, la, la, la, la, Bob - by Mc - Gee, yeah.

La, la, la, la, la, la. La, na, na, na, na.

1.-5.

La, na, la, la, la, la, Bob - by Mc - Gee, yeah. 2. La, la,

6.

(6.) Hey, hey, hey, Bob-by Mc-Gee, yeah.

Additional Lyrics

2. La, la, la, la, la, la, la, la, la, la, la, la,
La, la, la, la, la, la, la, la, lo,
Hey, now, Bobby, lo, na, Bobby McGee, yeah.
Lo, na, lo, na, na, lo, na, na,
Lo, na, na, la, na, na, la, na, na, la, na, na, la, na, na,
Hey, a now, Bobby, lo, na, Bobby McGee, yeah.

3. Lo, and I called him my lover, called him my man,
I said I called him my lover just the best I can. Come on.
And a Bobby now, and a Bobby McGee, yeah.
La, na, la, na, la, na, la, na, la, na, la, na, la, na, la, na.
Hey, hey, hey, Bobby McGee, lo.

Me and Julio Down by the Schoolyard

Words and Music by Paul Simon

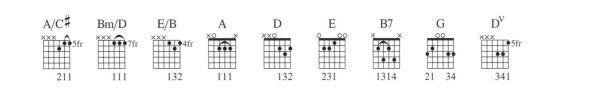

Copyright © 1971 Paul Simon (BMI)
International Copyright Secured   All Rights Reserved
Used by Permission

Oh, what the ma-ma saw, it was a-gainst the law. 2. Hoo,

% Verse

Ma-ma look down and spit on the ground ev-'ry time my name gets men - tioned. Pa-
3. *See additional lyrics*

- pa said, "Oy, if I get that boy, I'm gon-na stick him in a house of de-ten -

Chorus

- tion." 1. Well, I'm on my way, I don't know
3. And
2. *Whistle*

where I'm go - in' I'm on my way. I'm tak-in' my time, but I don't know where. Good-bye to

Ros - ie, the Queen of Co - ro - na. See

me and Ju - li - o down by the school yard. See

Additional Lyrics

2. Whoa, in a couple of days they come and take me away,
   But the press let the story leak.
   And when the radical Priest come to get me released,
   We was all on the cover of Newsweek.

Melissa

Words and Music by Gregg Allman and Steve Alaimo

Copyright © 1968 by Unichappell Music Inc., EMI Longitude Music and Elijah Blue Music
Copyright Renewed
International Copyright Secured   All Rights Reserved

bear - ing sor - row, ___ hav - ing fun, ___
There are no blan - kets ___ where he lies. ___
Or will his spir - it _____ fall a - way? _____

but back home _ you'll al - ways run   to sweet Mel-is - sa. ___
Lord, in the deep-est dreams the gypsy flies   with sweet Mel-is - sa. ___
But I know _ that he won't stay   with - out Mel-is - sa. ___

To Coda

Hmmm. ___

1.

2.

Bridge

A - gain the morn - in's come, ___   a - gain he's on the run. ___

Peace of Mind

Words and Music by Tom Scholz

1. Now if you're feel-in' kind-a low 'bout the dues you've been pay-ing,
fu-ture's com-in' much too slow.

2., 3. *See additional lyrics*

And you wan-na run but some-how you just keep on stay-in',
can't de-cide on which way to go, _____ whoa. ___ Yeah, yeah, yeah.

Copyright © 1976 Pure Songs
Copyright Renewed
All Rights Administered by Next Decade Entertainment, Inc.
All Rights Reserved   Used by Permission

Additional Lyrics

2. Now you're climbin' to the top of the company ladder,
   Hope it doesn't take too long.
   Can't ya see there'll come a day when it won't matter,
   Come a day when you'll be gone?

3. Now ev'rybody's got advice they just keep on givin',
   Doesn't mean too much to me.
   Lots of people out to make-believe they're livin',
   Can't decide who they should be.

Night Moves

Words and Music by Bob Seger

*Symbols in parentheses represent chord names respective to capoed guitar.
Symbols above reflect actual sounding chords.

1. I was a lit-tle too tall, could've used a few pounds.

Tight pants, points, hard-ly re-nown.

She was a black-haired beau-ty with big,
3. *See additional lyrics*

dark eyes, and points all her own sit-tin' way up high,

way up firm and high.

Copyright © 1976 Gear Publishing Co.
Copyright Renewed 2004
All Rights Reserved   Used by Permission

Additional Lyrics

3. We weren't in love, oh no, far from it.
We weren't searchin' for some pie in the sky summit.
We were just young and restless and bored,
Livin' by the sword.

4. And we'd steal away ev'ry chance we could
To the back room, to the alley, or the trusty woods.
I used her, she used me, but neither one cared.
We were gettin' our share.

Outro Night moves, yeah.
I remember, I sure remember the night moves.
Ain't it funny how you remember? Funny how you remember.
I remember, I remember, I remember, I remem..., oh, oh, oh.
We're workin', workin' and practicin'. Workin' and practicin'
All of the night moves, night moves, oh.
I remember, yeah, yeah, yeah, I remember, oo.
I remember, Lord, I remember, Lord, I remember, oh!
Oo, hoo. Ah, yeah, yeah, yeah, yeah.
Ah, huh. Ah, huh. I remember, I remember.

Peace Train

Words and Music by Cat Stevens

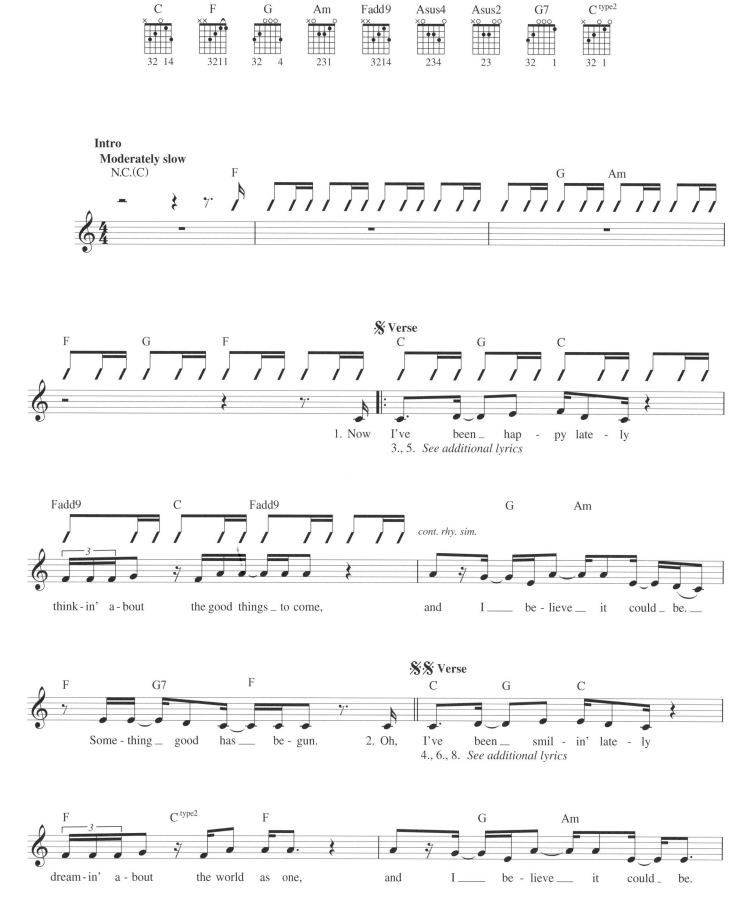

Copyright © 1971 (Renewed) Cat Music Limited
International Copyright Secured   All Rights Reserved
Reprinted by Permission of Music Sales Limited/Music Sales Corporation

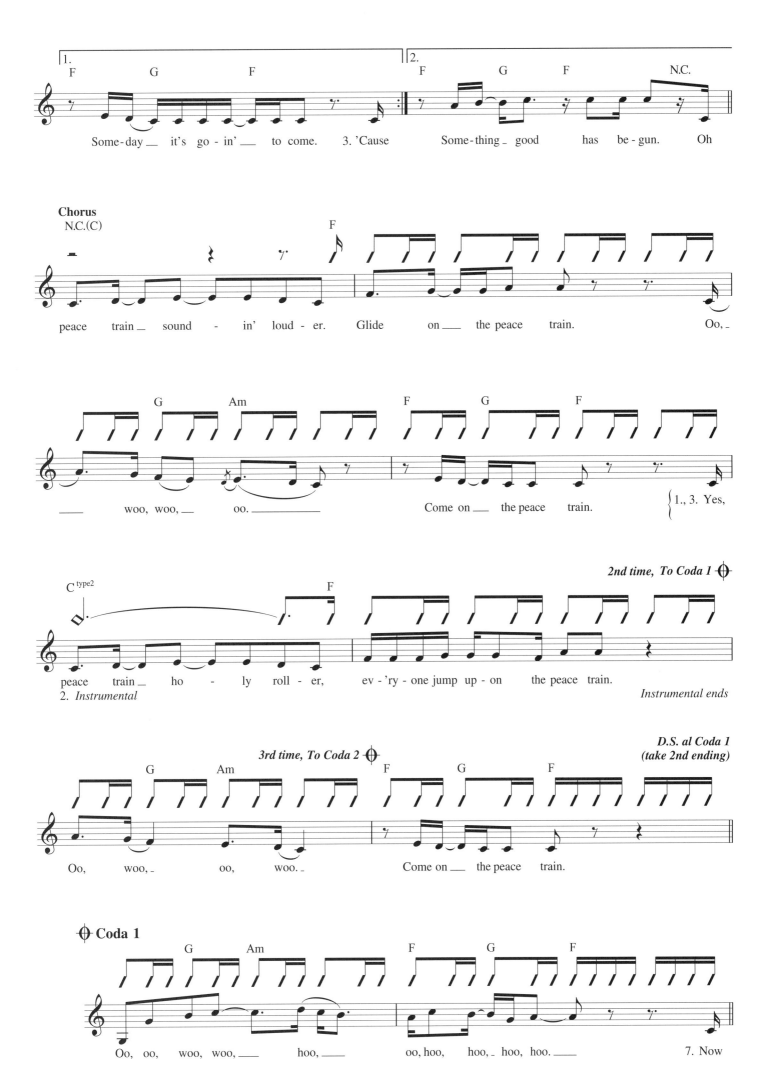

Verse

C   G   C   F   C^{type2}   F

I've been_ cry - in' late - ly_   think - in' a - bout   the world   as   it   is.

D.S.S. al Coda 2
(take 2nd ending)

G   Am   F   G   F

Why   must_ we go   on hat - ing?   Why can't_ we live   in bliss?   8. 'Cause

Coda 2

F   G   F   G   Am

(Come on,   come on,   come on.)   Yes, come   on_ peace _ train,   ay._

F   G   C^{type2}   F

Yes, it's_ the peace   train! _____

1.

G   Am   F   G   F

Come on _ the peace   train.   Oh, peace   train._

2.   **Outro**

G   Am   F   G   F

Oo,   woo, _   oo,   woo. _

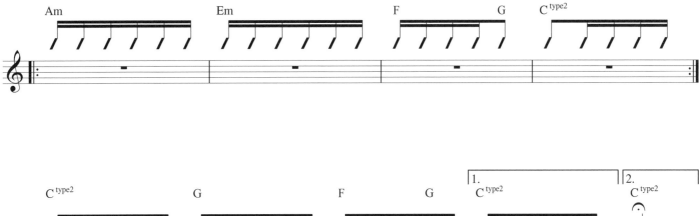

Additional Lyrics

3. 'Cause out on the edge of darkness
   There rides a peace train.
   Oh, peace train take this country,
   Come take me home again.

4. Now I've been smilin' lately,
   Thinkin' about the good things to come,
   And I believe it could be.
   Something good has begun.

5. Get your bags together,
   Go bring your good friends too.
   Because it's gettin' nearer,
   It soon will be with you.

6. Oh, come and join the living,
   It's not so far from you.
   And it's gettin' nearer.
   Soon it will all be true.

8. 'Cause out on the edge of darkness
   There rides a peace train.
   Oh, peace train take this country,
   Come take me home again.

Pinball Wizard

Words and Music by Peter Townshend

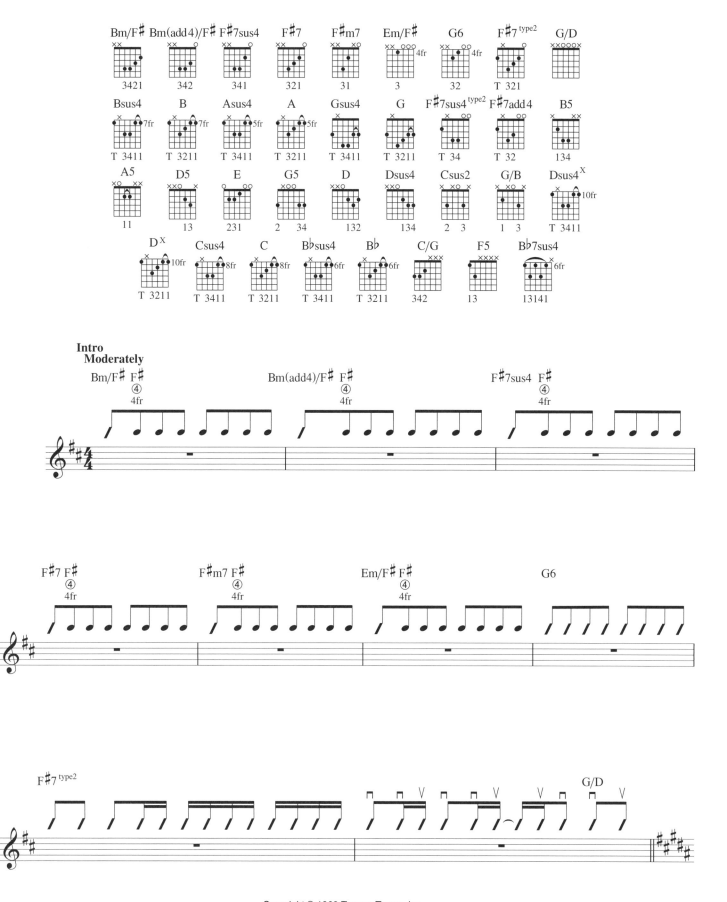

Copyright © 1969 Towser Tunes, Inc.,
Fabulous Music Ltd. and ABKCO Music, Inc.
Copyright Renewed
All Rights for Towser Tunes, Inc. Administered by
Universal Music Publishing International MGB Ltd.
All Rights for Universal Music Publishing International MGB Ltd. in the U.S.
Administered by Universal Music - Careers
International Copyright Secured   All Rights Reserved

He's a pin - ball wiz - ard. There has ___ to be a twist. A
I thought I was the Bal - ly ta - ble king, but

pin - ball wiz-ard's got such a sup - ple wrist. _____
I just hand - ed my pin - ball crown to him. _____

To Coda ⊕

Bridge

Gtr. 2 tacet

How do you think _ he does ___ it?
(I don't _ know.) _____

D.S. al Coda
(take 2nd ending)

⊕ **Coda**

Interlude

What makes him _ so good? _

4. E - ven

Additional Lyrics

2. He stands like a statue, becomes part of the machine.
   Feelin' all the bumpers, always playing clean.
   Plays by intuition, the digit counters fall.
   That deaf, dumb and blind kid sure plays a mean pinball.

3. Ain't got no distractions, can't hear no buzzers and bells.
   Don't see no lights a flashin', plays by sense of smell.
   Always gets a replay, never seen him fall.
   That deaf, dumb and blind kid sure plays a mean pinball.

Pink Houses

Words and Music by John Mellencamp

© 1983 EMI FULL KEEL MUSIC
All Rights Reserved   International Copyright Secured   Used by Permission

clean - ing up the eve - ning ___ slop. ___
"Boy you're gon - na be pres - i - dent."
but they ain't no big deal. ___

And he looks ___
But just like
'Cause the sim -

F ... **C/G**

at her and ___ says "Hey dar - lin',
ev - 'ry - thing else, those old cra - zy dreams

I can re-mem - ber when ___ you could ___
just kind of came and

G5 ... **Chorus** **C/G**

stop a clock." ___
went. ___

Oh, but ain't that A - mer - i - ca, for you and me. ___

G5 ... **C/G** ... **G5**

___ Ain't that A - mer - i - ca, some-thing to see, ___ ba - by. Ain't that A - mer -

C/G ... **D**

i - ca, home of the free, ___ yeah. ___ Lit - tle pink hous - es for

C/G ... **G** **B** **G** **G5**
⑥ ⑤ ③
3fr 2fr open

you and me. Oh, ___ yeah, for you and me. Ow.
Oh, ___ build them ba - by, for ___ you and me.

111

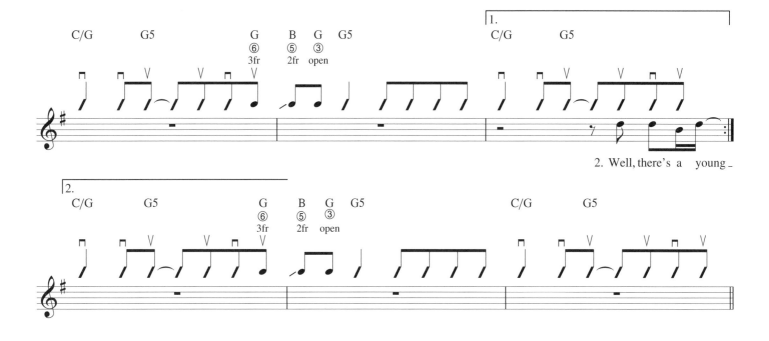

2. Well, there's a young

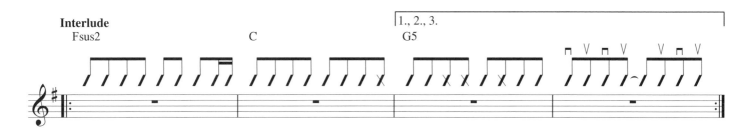

Interlude

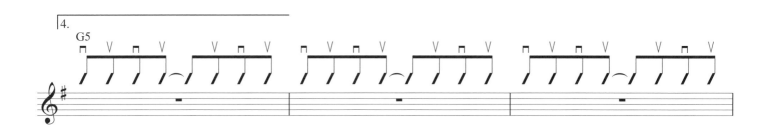

3. Well, there's peo -

- ple, man, ba - by, pays for the thrills, the bills, the

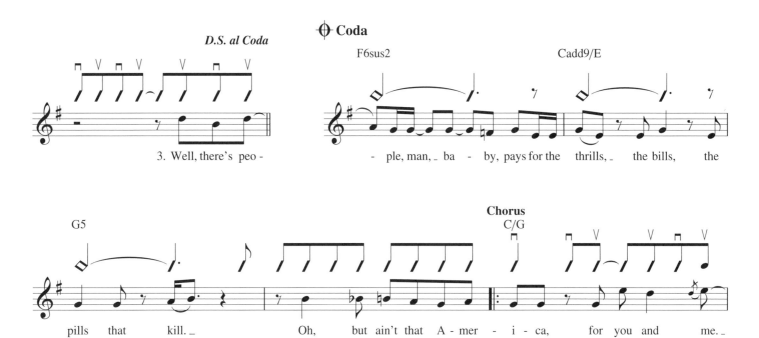

pills that kill. Oh, but ain't that A - mer - i - ca, for you and me.

Promises

Words and Music by Richard Feldman and Roger Linn

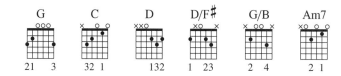

Copyright © 1978 by Narwhal Music (BMI)
International Copyright Secured   All Rights Reserved

I got a wom - an   call - in' love   hate. _____
I got a wom - an   cal - lin' love   hate. _____

We made a vow ___   we'd al - ways be friends. ___   How could we

know that prom - i - ses _____ end?   **Chorus**   La   la,   la,   la,   la,   la, ___   la, ___

la.   La,   la,   la,   la,   la, ___   la, ___   la.

La,

Outro   *Repeat and fade*

la,   la,   la,   la, ___   la,   la.   La,
Whoa, _

116

Rocket Man
(I Think It's Gonna Be a Long Long Time)

Words and Music by Elton John and Bernie Taupin

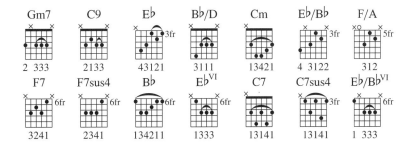

Verse
Moderately slow

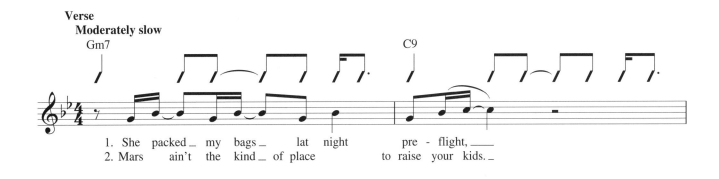

1. She packed _ my bags _ lat night pre - flight, ___
2. Mars ain't the kind _ of place to raise your kids. _

ze - ro hour ____ nine A. M. _____
In fact, _ it's cold _ as hell. _____

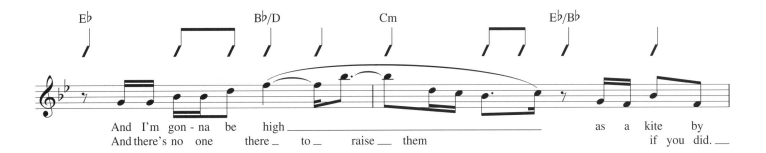

And I'm gon - na be high _____ as a kite by
And there's no one there _ to _ raise _ them if you did. __

Copyright © 1972 UNIVERSAL/DICK JAMES MUSIC LTD.
Copyright Renewed
All Rights in the United States and Canada Controlled and Administered by
UNIVERSAL - SONGS OF POLYGRAM INTERNATIONAL, INC.
All Rights Reserved   Used by Permission

then.

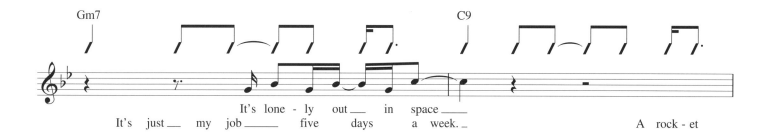

I miss the earth so much; I miss my wife.
And all this sci - ence I don't un - der - stand.

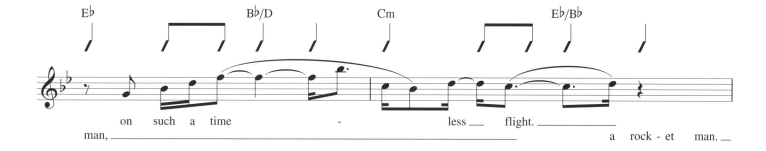

It's lone - ly out in space
It's just my job five days a week. A rock - et

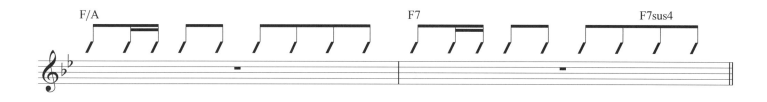

on such a time - less flight.
man, a rock - et man.

—

(Sittin' On)
The Dock of the Bay

Words and Music by Steve Cropper and Otis Redding

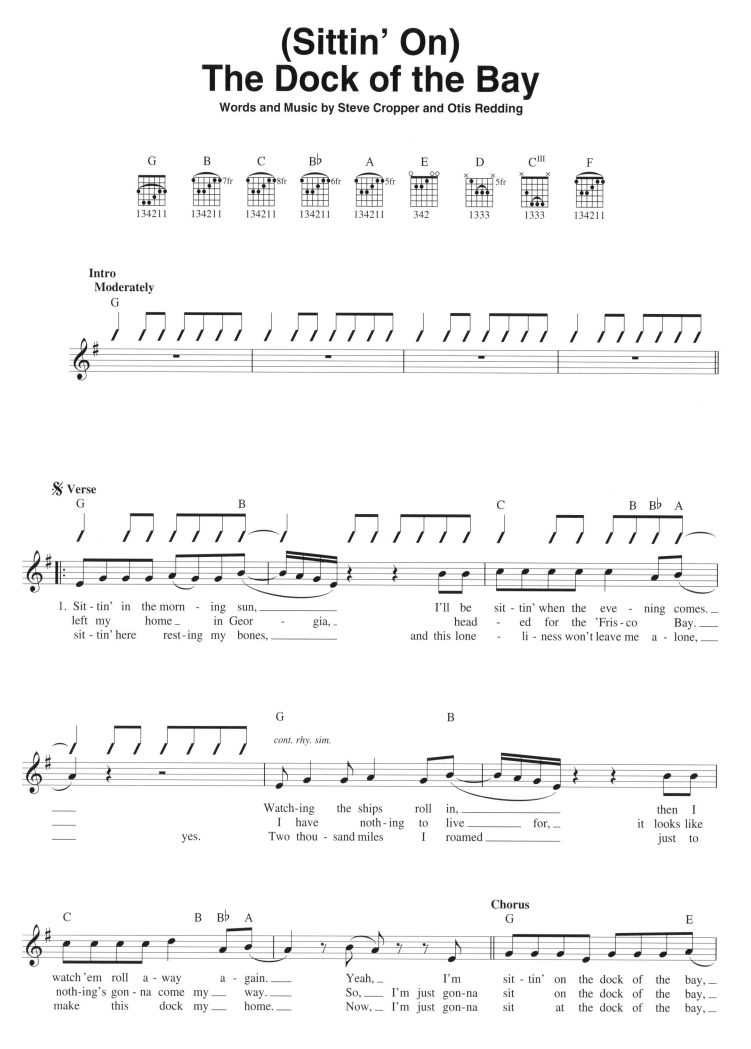

Copyright © 1968, 1975 IRVING MUSIC, INC.
Copyright Renewed
All Rights Reserved   Used by Permission

Southern Cross

Words and Music by Stephen Stills, Richard Curtis and Michael Curtis

Copyright © 1974, 1982 Gold Hill Music, Inc. and Three Wise Boys Music LLC
Copyright Renewed
All Rights Reserved   Used by Permission

125

Space Oddity

Words and Music by David Bowie

© Copyright 1969 (Renewed) Onward Music Ltd., London, England
TRO - Essex Music International, Inc., New York, controls all publication rights for the U.S.A. and Canada
International Copyright Secured
All Rights Reserved Including Public Performance For Profit
Used by Permission

℅ Chorus

Fmaj7   Em

here   am   I   sit-ting in a   tin can, _____
                       float-ing 'round my

Fmaj7   Em   B♭   Am   G

cont. rhy. sim.

far _____ a-bove _ the   world. _   Plan-et Earth _ is   blue,   and there's   noth-ing   I can
                moon. _

F   **Interlude**
                                     C   E   F   G^III   E   A
                                    ⑥   ⑥
                                   open   open

do.

To Coda ⊕

Guitar Solo

C   E   F   G^III   E   A   Fmaj7
⑥   ⑥
open   open

Em7   A^open

C^open   D/E   E

Verse

C/G   E7

3. Though I'm   past one hun - dred thou-sand miles, _____   I'm   feel-ing ver - y still. _

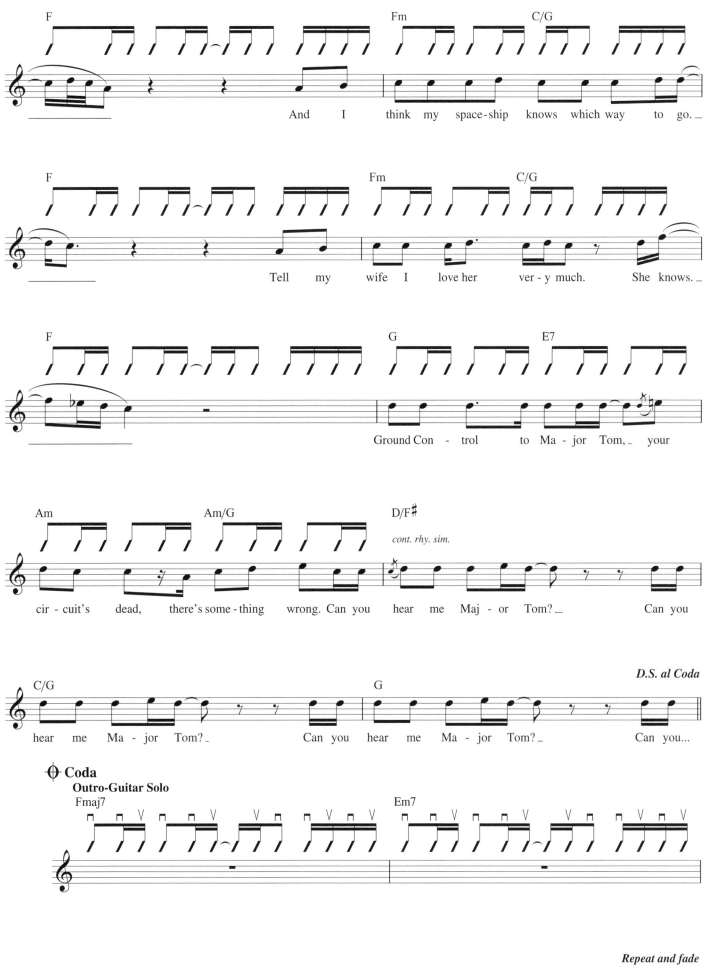

Stuck in the Middle with You

Words and Music by Gerry Rafferty and Joe Egan

Copyright © 1973; Renewed 2001 Stage Three Songs (ASCAP) o/b/o Stage Three Music Ltd. (PRS)
and Baby Bun Music Ltd. (PRS)
Worldwide Rights for Stage Three Songs Administered by BMG Gold Songs
International Copyright Secured   All Rights Reserved

Tangled Up in Blue

Words and Music by Bob Dylan

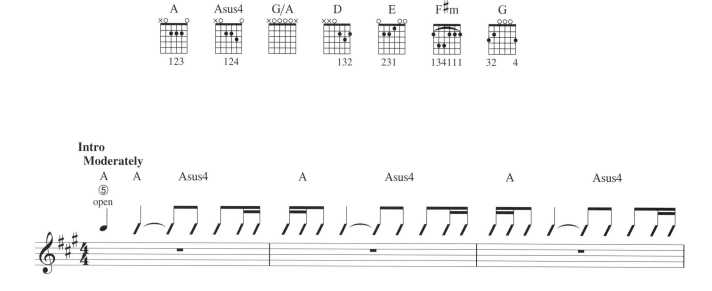

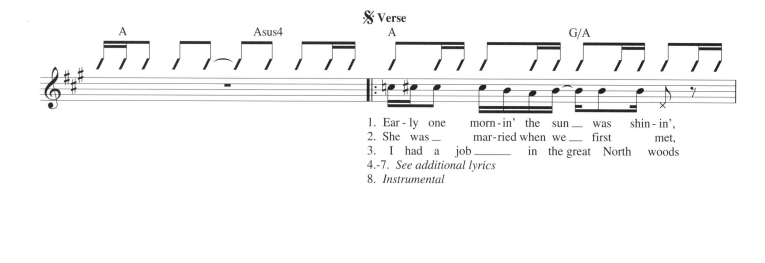

1. Ear - ly one   morn-in' the sun __ was   shin - in',
2. She was __   mar-ried when we __ first   met,
3. I had a   job _____ in the great North   woods
4.-7. *See additional lyrics*
8. *Instrumental*

I was   lay - in' in bed, _   won - d'rin' if __ she's _ changed   at   all, ___ if her
      soon to be di - vorced. _   I helped her out of a   jam _ I   guess, _ but I
work - in' as a cook for a   spell.   But I   nev - er did like _ it all _____ that   much, _ and one

Copyright © 1974, 1976 Ram's Horn Music
International Copyright Secured   All Rights Reserved

hair   was _ still   red. ___
used a   lit - tle too much   force. _
day   the axe _ just _ fell. ___

Her folks, they said our   lives _ to - geth - er
We   drove that   car   as   far as we could, _   a -
So I   drift - ed down ____   to New Or - leans, _ where I,

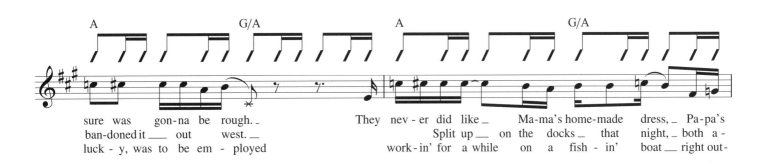

sure was   gon - na be rough. __
ban - doned it ___ out   west. __
luck - y, was to be em - ployed

They nev - er did like _   Ma - ma's home - made   dress, _ Pa - pa's
Split up _ on the docks _ that   night, _ both a -
work - in' for a while   on a fish - in'   boat _ right out -

bank book was - n't big e - nough. __
gree - ing it ___ was _ best. __
- side   of _ Del - a - croix. _

And   I was stand - in' on the side of the road, _   rain _
As   she turned a - round ___ to look at _ me, _ as I ___
But all   the while ___ I was a - lone, ____ the past _

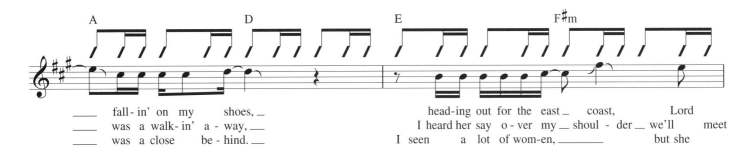

____ fall - in' on my   shoes, _
____ was a walk - in' a - way, _
____ was a close   be - hind. __

head - ing out for the east _ coast,   Lord
I heard her say o - ver my _ shoul - der _ we'll   meet
I seen   a lot of wom - en, _____ but she

To Coda

knows I've paid some dues _ get - tin' through _
_ a - gain _ some-day _ on the av - e - nue _____
nev - er 'scaped my mind _ and I just grew

tan - gled up in blue. _____

7th time, D.S. al Coda

Play 7 times

Coda

rit.

Additional Lyrics

4. She was working in topless place
   And I stopped in for a beer.
   I just kept looking at the side of her face
   In the spotlight so clear.
   And later on when the crowd thinned out
   I was just about to do the same.
   She was standing there in back of my chair,
   Said to me, "Don't I know your name?"
   I muttered something underneath my breath.
   She studied the lines on my face.
   I must admit I felt a little uneasy
   When she bent down to tie the laces of my shoe,
   Tangled up in blue.

5. She lit a burner on the stove
   And offered me a pipe.
   "I thought you'd never say hello," she said.
   "You look like the silent type."
   Then she opened up a book of poems
   And handed it to me,
   Written by an Italian poet
   From the thirteenth century.
   And every one of them words rang true
   And glowed like burning coal,
   Pourin' off of every page
   Like it was written in my soul,
   From me to you,
   Tangled up in blue.

6. I lived with them on Montague Street
   In a basement down the stairs.
   There was music in the cafes at night
   And revolution in the air.
   Then he started in the dealing with slaves
   And something inside of him died.
   She had to sell everything she owned
   And froze up inside.
   And when it fin'lly, the bottom fell out,
   I became withdrawn.
   The only thing I knew how to do
   Was to keep on keeping on,
   Like a bird that flew
   Tangled up in blue.

7. So now I'm going back again.
   I got to get to her somehow.
   All the people we used to know,
   They're an illusion to me now.
   Some are math'maticians,
   Some are carpenters' wives.
   Don't know how it all got started,
   I don't know what they do with their lives.
   But me, I'm still on the road
   Headin' for another joint.
   We always did feel the same,
   We just saw it from a different point of view,
   Tangled up in blue.

Thick As a Brick

Words and Music by Ian Anderson

Capo III

*Symbols in parentheses represent chord names respective to capoed guitar.
Symbols above reflect actual sounding chords.

1. Real-ly don't mind ___ if you sit this one ___ out. ___ My ___ word's but a whis-per, a deaf-ness, a shout. I ___ may make you feel ___ that I can't ___ make you think. Your ___ sperm's in the gut-ter, your love's ___

___ sand-cas-tle vir-tues ___ are all swept a-way in the tid-al de-struc-tion, ___ the mor-al me-lee. The e-las-tic re-treat ___ rings ___ the close ___ of play. As the last wave ___ un-cov-ers ___ the

Copyright © 1976 Chrysalis Music Ltd.
Copyright Renewed
All Rights for the U.S. and Canada Administered by Chrysalis Music
All Rights Reserved   Used by Permission

Wasted on the Way

Words and Music by Graham Nash

Copyright © 1982 Nash Notes
All Rights Administered by Sony/ATV Music Publishing LLC, 8 Music Square West, Nashville, TN 37203
International Copyright Secured   All Rights Reserved

ques - tion all ___ the an - swers? Did you en - vy all ___ the danc-

-ers who had all the nerve? Look a - round you now.

You must go for what ___ you want - ed. Look at all my friends who

did and got what they de - served. So much

time to make up ev - 'ry - where ___ you turn, _____

time we have wast - ed on ___ the way. _____

So much wa - ter mov - ing un - der - neath ___ the bridge. _____

140

We Just Disagree

Words and Music by Jim Krueger

© 1976, 1977 (Renewed 2004, 2005) EMI BLACKWOOD MUSIC INC. and BRUISER MUSIC
All Rights Controlled and Administered by EMI BLACKWOOD MUSIC INC.
All Rights Reserved   International Copyright Secured   Used by Permission

The Weight

By J.R. Robertson

1. I pulled in-to Na-za-reth, was feel-in''bout half-past dead.
2.-5. *See additional lyrics*

I just need some-place _ where I __ can lay __ my head. _

"Hey, mis-ter, can you tell me where a man __ might find a bed?" _

He just grinned and shook my hand; _ "No" __ was all __ he said.

Copyright © 1968, 1974 (Renewed) Dwarf Music
International Copyright Secured   All Rights Reserved
Reprinted by Permission of Music Sales Corporation

Chorus

Take a load off Fan - ny, take a load for free.

Take a load off Fan - ny and you put the load right on me.

To Coda | 1., 2., 3. | | 4. |

D.S. al Coda

Coda

Additional Lyrics

2. I picked up my bag; I went looking for a place to hide
When I saw Carmen and the Devil walking side by side.
I said, "Hey, Carmen, come on, let's go down town."
She said, "I gotta go, but my friend can stick around."

3. Go down, Miss Moses, there's nothing you can say.
It's just ol' Luke, and Luke's waiting on the judgement day.
"Well, Luke, my friend, what about young Anna Lee?"
He said, "Do me a favour, son, won't you stay
And keep Anna Lee company?"

4. Crazy Chester followed me, and he caught me in the fog.
He said, "I'll fix your rack if you'll take Jack, my dog."
I said, "Wait a minute, Chester, you know I'm a peaceful man."
He said, "That's O.K., boy, won't you feed him when you can?"

5. Catch a cannonball now, to take me down the line.
My bag is sinking low, and I do believe it's time
To get back to Miss Fanny, you know she's the only one
Who sent me here with her regards for everyone.

Who'll Stop the Rain

Words and Music by John Fogerty

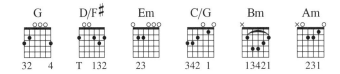

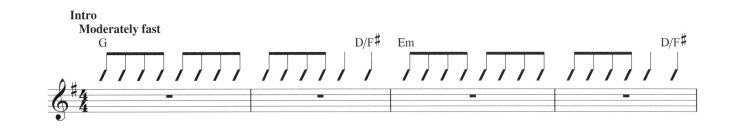

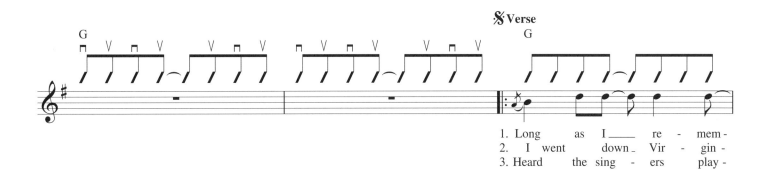

1. Long as I ___ re - mem -
2. I went down ___ Vir - gin -
3. Heard the sing - ers play -

- ber, the rain ___ been com - in' down. ___ Clouds of mys - t'ry pour -
- ia seek - in' shel - ter from ___ the storm. ___ Caught up in ___ the fa -
- ing, how ___ we cheered ___ for more. ___ The crowd had rushed ___ to-geth -

- in' ___ con - fu - sion on ___ the ground. ___ Good men through ___ the a - ges ___
- ble, ___ I watched ___ the tow - er grow. ___ Five year plans ___ and new deals ___
- er, ___ try - in' to ___ keep warm. ___ Still the rain ___ kept pour - in', ___

*2nd & 3rd times, substitute Bm

Copyright © 1970 Jondora Music
Copyright Renewed
International Copyright Secured All Rights Reserved

try - in' to find __ the sun; ___
wrapped in gold - en chains; _
fall - in' on __ my ears; ___

and I won - der, still I won - der

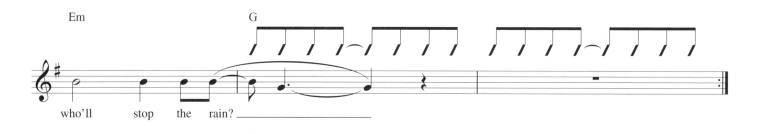

who'll stop the rain? ___

Interlude

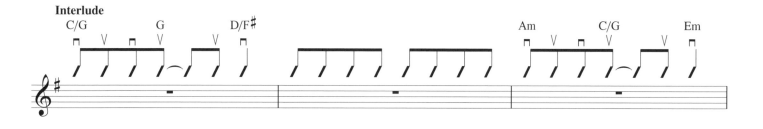

D.S. al Coda

⊕ **Coda**

who'll stop the rain? ___

Outro

Repeat and fade

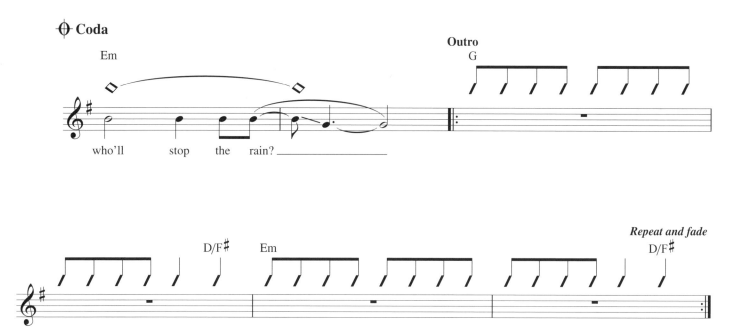

147

Working Class Hero

Words and Music by John Lennon

Copyright © 1970 Yoko Ono, Sean Lennon and Julian Lennon
Copyright Renewed
All Rights Administered by Sony/ATV Music Publishing LLC,
8 Music Square West, Nashville, TN 37203
International Copyright Secured   All Rights Reserved

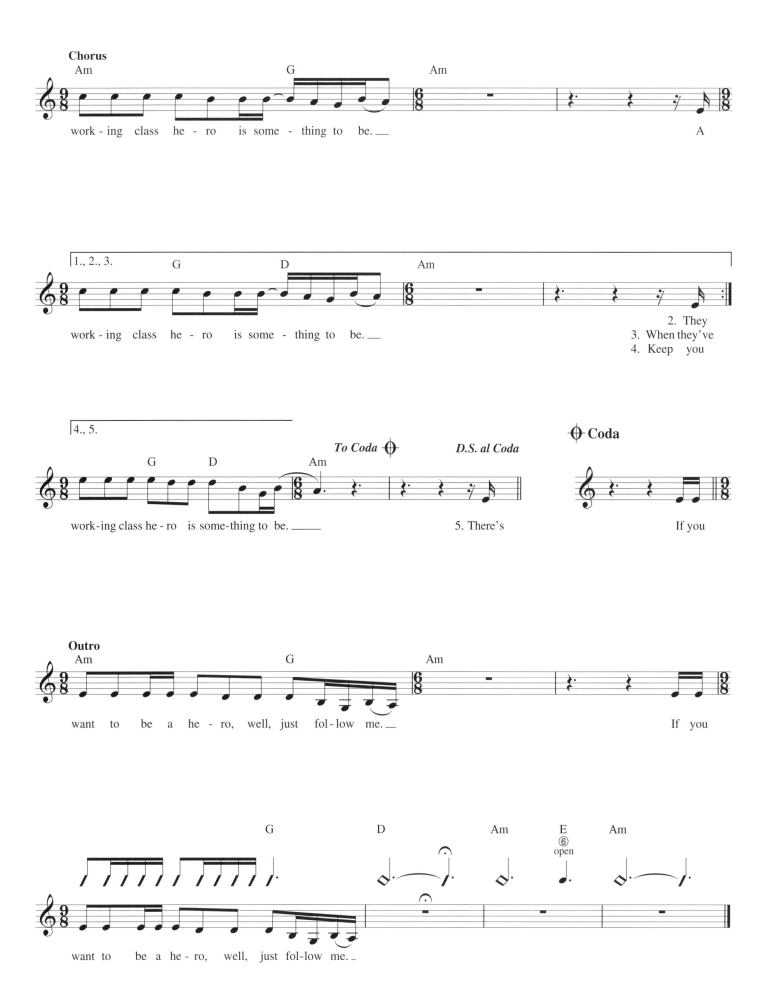

Additional Lyrics

4. Keep you doped with religion and sex and TV.
   And you think you're so clever and classless and free.
   But you're still fucking peasants as far as I can see.

5. There's room at the top they are telling you still.
   But first you must learn how to smile as you kill
   If you want to be like the folks on the hill.

You've Got to Hide Your Love Away

Words and Music by John Lennon and Paul McCartney

Intro
Moderately

1. Here I stand, head in hand,
2. *See additional lyrics*
3. *Instrumental*

turn my face to the wall. ___ If she's gone, I

To Coda

cont. rhy. sim.

can't go on, ___ feel - ing two foot small. ___

cont. rhy. sim.

Ev - 'ry - where peo - ple ___ stare, ___ each and ___ ev - 'ry - day. ___

___ I can see them laugh at ___ me,

Copyright © 1965 Sony/ATV Music Publishing LLC
Copyright Renewed
All Rights Administered by Sony/ATV Music Publishing LLC, 8 Music Square West, Nashville, TN 37203
International Copyright Secured   All Rights Reserved

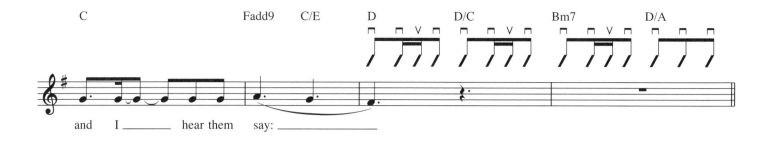

and I _____ hear them say: _____

Chorus

Hey! __ You've got to hide your __ love a - way. _____

cont. rhy. sim.

Hey! __ You've got to hide your __ love a -

2nd time, D.S. al Coda

Coda

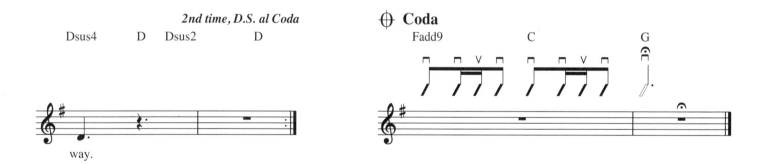

way.

Additional Lyrics

2. How can I even try, I can never win.
Hearing them, seeing them, in the state I'm in.
How could she say to me love will find a way?
Gather 'round all you clowns, let me hear you say:

Time for Me to Fly

Words and Music by Kevin Cronin

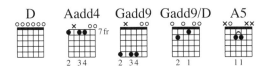

Open D tuning:
(low to high) D–A–D–G–B–D

Copyright © 1978 Fate Music (ASCAP)
International Copyright Secured All Rights Reserved

feel-in' I know_ is gone._ I do be-lieve that I've _ had e - nough._ I've had e-

nough of the false-ness _ of a worn - out re-la - tion._ E-nough of the jeal - ous-y ___ and the

in - tol - er-a - tion._ Oh, I make you laugh ___ and a you make me cry. ___

I be-lieve it's time _ for me _ to fly. _____ (Time for me _ to fly _

Chorus

Oh, I've got to set ___ my - self free. ___ Ah, that's just how it's a
Oh, _____ ba - by, that's _ just how it's a

_____ ee i. ___ Time for me _ to fly, _____

got to ___ be. ___

got to ___ be. ___ Oh, ___ I know it hurts _ to say _ good - bye, _ but it's time for me _ to fly. _

oo. ___

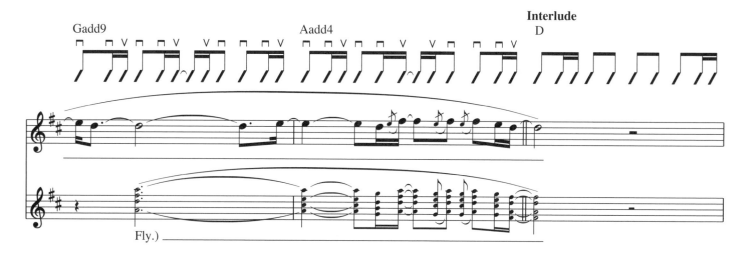

Interlude

Fly.) ___

Oo, ___ ba -

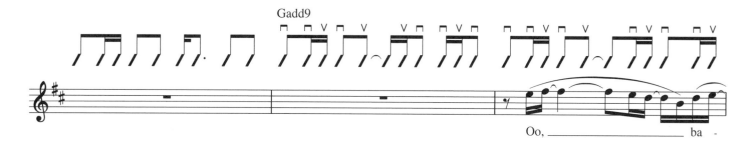

by.

D.S. al Coda

Well, don't you know it's time for me _ to fly. ___

155

AUTHENTIC CHORDS · ORIGINAL KEYS · COMPLETE SONGS

The *Strum It* series lets players strum the chords and sing along with their favorite hits. Each song has been selected because it can be played with regular open chords, barre chords, or other moveable chord types. Guitarists can simply play the rhythm, or play and sing along through the entire song. All songs are shown in their original keys complete with chords, strum patterns, melody and lyrics. Wherever possible, the chord voicings from the recorded versions are notated.

ACOUSTIC CLASSICS
_____ 00699238.........................$10.95

THE BEACH BOYS' GREATEST HITS
_____ 00699357.........................$12.95

THE BEATLES FAVORITES
_____ 00699249.........................$14.95

BEST OF CONTEMPORARY CHRISTIAN
_____ 00699531.........................$12.95

BEST OF STEVEN CURTIS CHAPMAN
_____ 00699530.........................$12.95

VERY BEST OF JOHNNY CASH
_____ 00699514.........................$14.99

CELTIC GUITAR SONGBOOK
_____ 00699265.........................$9.95

CHRISTMAS SONGS FOR GUITAR
_____ 00699247.........................$10.95

CHRISTMAS SONGS WITH 3 CHORDS
_____ 00699487.........................$8.95

VERY BEST OF ERIC CLAPTON
_____ 00699560.........................$12.95

COUNTRY STRUMMIN'
_____ 00699119.........................$8.95

JIM CROCE – CLASSIC HITS
_____ 00699269.........................$10.95

VERY BEST OF JOHN DENVER
_____ 00699488.........................$12.95

NEIL DIAMOND
_____ 00699593.........................$12.95

DISNEY FAVORITES
_____ 00699171.........................$10.95

BEST OF THE DOORS
_____ 00699177.........................$12.99

MELISSA ETHERIDGE GREATEST HITS
_____ 00699518.........................$12.99

FAVORITE SONGS WITH 3 CHORDS
_____ 00699112.........................$8.95

FAVORITE SONGS WITH 4 CHORDS
_____ 00699270.........................$8.95

FIRESIDE SING-ALONG
_____ 00699273.........................$8.95

FOLK FAVORITES
_____ 00699517.........................$8.95

IRVING BERLIN'S GOD BLESS AMERICA®
_____ 00699508.........................$9.95

GREAT '50s ROCK
_____ 00699187.........................$9.95

GREAT '60s ROCK
_____ 00699188.........................$9.95

GREAT '70s ROCK
_____ 00699262.........................$9.95

THE GUITAR STRUMMERS' ROCK SONGBOOK
_____ 00701678.........................$14.99

BEST OF WOODY GUTHRIE
_____ 00699496.........................$12.95

JOHN HIATT COLLECTION
_____ 00699398.........................$12.95

THE VERY BEST OF BOB MARLEY
_____ 00699524.........................$12.95

A MERRY CHRISTMAS SONGBOOK
_____ 00699211.........................$9.95

MORE FAVORITE SONGS WITH 3 CHORDS
_____ 00699532.........................$8.95

THE VERY BEST OF TOM PETTY
_____ 00699336.........................$12.95

POP-ROCK GUITAR FAVORITES
_____ 00699088.........................$8.95

ELVIS! GREATEST HITS
_____ 00699276.........................$10.95

SONGS FOR KIDS
_____ 00699616.........................$9.95

BEST OF GEORGE STRAIT
_____ 00699235.........................$14.99

25 COUNTRY STANDARDS
_____ 00699523.........................$12.95

BEST OF HANK WILLIAMS JR.
_____ 00699224.........................$12.95

HAL•LEONARD®
7777 W. BLUEMOUND RD. P.O. BOX 13819 MILWAUKEE, WI 53213

Visit Hal Leonard online at **www.halleonard.com**

Prices, contents & availability subject to change without notice.

0811

Guitar Chord Songbooks

Each 6" x 9" book includes complete lyrics, chord symbols, and guitar chord diagrams.

Acoustic Rock
00699540 . . . . $17.95

Alabama
00699914 . . . . $14.95

The Beach Boys
00699566 . . . . $14.95

The Beatles (A-I)
00699558 . . . . $17.99

The Beatles (J-Y)
00699562 . . . . $17.99

Blues
00699733 . . . . $12.95

Broadway
00699920 . . . . $14.99

Johnny Cash
00699648 . . . . $16.95

Steven Curtis Chapman
00700702 . . . . $17.99

Children's Songs
00699539 . . . . $14.95

Christmas Carols
00699536 . . . . $12.95

Christmas Songs
00699537 . . . . $12.95

Eric Clapton
00699567 . . . . $15.99

Classic Rock
00699598 . . . . $15.99

Contemporary Christian
00699564 . . . . $14.95

Country
00699534 . . . . $14.95

Country Favorites
00700609 . . . . $14.99

Country Standards
00700608 . . . . $12.95

Cowboy Songs
00699636 . . . . $12.95

Crosby, Stills & Nash
00701609 . . . . $12.99

Neil Diamond
00700606 . . . . $14.99

Disney
00701071 . . . . $14.99

The Doors
00699888 . . . . $15.99

Early Rock
00699916 . . . . $14.99

Folksongs
00699541 . . . . $12.95

Folk Pop Rock
00699651 . . . . $14.95

Four Chord Songs
00701611 . . . . $12.99

Gospel Hymns
00700463 . . . . $14.99

Grand Ole Opry®
00699885 . . . . $16.95

Hillsong United
00700222 . . . . $12.95

Irish Songs
00701044 . . . . $14.99

Jazz Standards
00700972 . . . . $14.99

Billy Joel
00699632 . . . . $15.99

Elton John
00699732 . . . . $15.99

Latin Songs
00700973 . . . . $14.99

Love Songs
00701043 . . . . $14.99

Paul McCartney
00385035 . . . . $16.95

Steve Miller
00701146 . . . . $12.99

Motown
00699734 . . . . $16.95

The 1950s
00699922 . . . . $14.99

The 1980s
00700551 . . . . $16.99

Nirvana
00699762 . . . . $16.99

Roy Orbison
00699752 . . . . $12.95

Tom Petty
00699883 . . . . $15.99

Pop/Rock
00699538 . . . . $14.95

Praise & Worship
00699634 . . . . $12.95

Elvis Presley
00699633 . . . . $14.95

Red Hot Chili Peppers
00699710 . . . . $16.95

Rock Ballads
00701034 . . . . $14.99

Rock 'n' Roll
00699535 . . . . $14.95

Bob Seger
00701147 . . . . $12.99

Taylor Swift
00701799 . . . . $14.99

Sting
00699921 . . . . $14.99

Three Chord Songs
00699720 . . . . $12.95

Wedding Songs
00701005 . . . . $14.99

Hank Williams
00700607 . . . . $14.99

FOR MORE INFORMATION, SEE YOUR LOCAL MUSIC DEALER,
OR WRITE TO:

HAL•LEONARD®
CORPORATION
7777 W. BLUEMOUND RD. P.O. BOX 13819 MILWAUKEE, WI 53213

Visit Hal Leonard online at **www.halleonard.com**

Prices, contents, and availability subject to change without notice.

THE BOOK SERIES
FOR EASY GUITAR

THE ACOUSTIC BOOK
00702251 Easy Guitar $16.99

THE BEATLES BOOK
00699266 Easy Guitar $19.95

THE BLUES BOOK – 2ND ED.
00702104 Easy Guitar $16.95

THE BROADWAY BOOK
00702015 Easy Guitar $17.95

THE CHRISTMAS CAROLS BOOK
00702186 Easy Guitar $14.95

THE CHRISTMAS CLASSICS BOOK
00702200 Easy Guitar $14.95

THE ERIC CLAPTON BOOK
00702056 Easy Guitar $18.95

THE CLASSIC COUNTRY BOOK
00702018 Easy Guitar $19.95

THE CLASSIC ROCK BOOK
00698977 Easy Guitar $19.95

THE CONTEMPORARY CHRISTIAN BOOK
00702195 Easy Guitar $16.95

THE COUNTRY CLASSIC FAVORITES BOOK
00702238 Easy Guitar $19.99

THE DISNEY SONGS BOOK
00702168 Easy Guitar $19.95

THE FOLKSONGS BOOK
00702180 Easy Guitar $14.95

THE GOSPEL SONGS BOOK
00702157 Easy Guitar $15.95

THE HARD ROCK BOOK
00702181 Easy Guitar $16.95

THE HYMN BOOK
00702142 Easy Guitar $14.99

THE JAZZ STANDARDS BOOK
00702164 Easy Guitar $15.95

THE LOVE SONGS BOOK
00702064 Easy Guitar $16.95

THE NEW COUNTRY HITS BOOK
00702017 Easy Guitar $19.95

THE ELVIS BOOK
00702163 Easy Guitar $19.95

THE R&B BOOK
0702058 Easy Guitar $16.95

THE ROCK CLASSICS BOOK
00702055 Easy Guitar $18.95

THE WEDDING SONGS BOOK
00702167 Easy Guitar $16.95

THE WORSHIP BOOK
00702247 Easy Guitar $14.99

FOR MORE INFORMATION, SEE YOUR LOCAL MUSIC DEALER,
OR WRITE TO:

HAL•LEONARD®
CORPORATION
7777 W. BLUEMOUND RD. P.O. BOX 13819 MILWAUKEE, WI 53213

www.halleonard.com

Prices, contents, and availablilty subject
to change without notice.

Disney characters and artwork © Disney Enterprises, Inc.

Get Better at Guitar

...with these Great Guitar Instruction Books from Hal Leonard!

101 GUITAR TIPS
INCLUDES TAB

STUFF ALL THE PROS
KNOW AND USE
by Adam St. James
This book contains invaluable
guidance on everything from scales
and music theory to truss rod
adjustments, proper recording
studio set-ups, and much more.
The book also features snippets of
advice from some of the most celebrated guitarists and
producers in the music business, including B.B. King, Steve
Vai, Joe Satriani, Warren Haynes, Laurence Juber, Pete
Anderson, Tom Dowd and others, culled from the author's
hundreds of interviews.
00695737 Book/CD Pack..$16.95

AMAZING PHRASING
INCLUDES TAB

50 WAYS TO IMPROVE YOUR
IMPROVISATIONAL SKILLS
by Tom Kolb
This book/CD pack explores all the
main components necessary for
crafting well-balanced rhythmic
and melodic phrases. It also explains
how these phrases are put together
to form cohesive solos. Many styles are covered – rock,
blues, jazz, fusion, country, Latin, funk and more – and all
of the concepts are backed up with musical examples. The
companion CD contains 89 demos for listening, and most
tracks feature full-band backing.
00695583 Book/CD Pack..$19.95

BLUES YOU CAN USE
INCLUDES TAB

by John Ganapes
A comprehensive source designed
to help guitarists develop both lead
and rhythm playing. Covers: Texas,
Delta, R&B, early rock and roll,
gospel, blues/rock and more.
Includes: 21 complete solos • chord
progressions and riffs • turnarounds
• moveable scales and more. CD features leads and full
band backing.
00695007 Book/CD Pack..$19.95

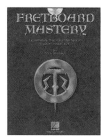

FRETBOARD MASTERY
INCLUDES TAB

by Troy Stetina
Untangle the mysterious regions of
the guitar fretboard and unlock
your potential. *Fretboard Mastery*
familiarizes you with all the shapes
you need to know by applying them
in real musical examples, thereby
reinforcing and reaffirming your
newfound knowledge. The result is a much higher level of
comprehension and retention.
00695331 Book/CD Pack..$19.95

FRETBOARD ROADMAPS – 2ND EDITION

ESSENTIAL GUITAR PATTERNS THAT
ALL THE PROS KNOW AND USE
by Fred Sokolow
The updated edition of this bestseller
features more songs, updated lessons,
and a full audio CD! Learn to play
lead and rhythm anywhere on the fretboard, in any key; play
a variety of lead guitar styles; play chords and progressions
anywhere on the fretboard; expand your chord vocabulary;
and learn to think musically – the way the pros do.
00695941 Book/CD Pack..$14.95

GUITAR AEROBICS
INCLUDES TAB

A 52-WEEK, ONE-LICK-PER-DAY
WORKOUT PROGRAM FOR
DEVELOPING, IMPROVING &
MAINTAINING GUITAR TECHNIQUE
by Troy Nelson
From the former editor of *Guitar
One* magazine, here is a daily dose
of vitamins to keep your chops fine
tuned! Musical styles include rock, blues, jazz, metal, country,
and funk. Techniques taught include alternate picking, arpeggios,
sweep picking, string skipping, legato, string bending, and
rhythm guitar. These exercises will increase speed, and
improve dexterity and pick- and fret-hand accuracy. The
accompanying CD includes all 365 workout licks plus play-along
grooves in every style at eight different metronome settings.
00695946 Book/CD Pack..$19.95

GUITAR CLUES
INCLUDES TAB

OPERATION PENTATONIC
by Greg Koch
Join renowned guitar master Greg
Koch as he clues you in to a wide
variety of fun and valuable pentatonic
scale applications. Whether you're
new to improvising or have been
doing it for a while, this book/CD
pack will provide loads of delicious licks and tricks that you
can use right away, from volume swells and chicken pickin'
to intervallic and chordal ideas. The CD includes 65 demo
and play-along tracks.
00695827 Book/CD Pack..$19.95

INTRODUCTION TO GUITAR TONE & EFFECTS

by David M. Brewster
This book/CD pack teaches the
basics of guitar tones and effects,
with audio examples on CD. Readers
will learn about: overdrive,
distortion and fuzz • using
equalizers • modulation effects •
reverb and delay • multi-effect processors • and more.
00695766 Book/CD Pack..$14.95

PICTURE CHORD ENCYCLOPEDIA

This comprehensive guitar chord
resource for all playing styles and
levels features five voicings of 44
chord qualities for all twelve keys –
2,640 chords in all! For each, there
is a clearly illustrated chord frame,
as well as *an actual photo* of the
chord being played! Includes info
on basic fingering principles, open chords and barre
chords, partial chords and broken-set forms, and more.
00695224 ....$19.95

SCALE CHORD RELATIONSHIPS
INCLUDES TAB

*by Michael Mueller &
Jeff Schroedl*
This book teaches players how to
determine which scales to play with
which chords, so guitarists will
never have to fear chord changes
again! This book/CD pack explains
how to: recognize keys • analyze
chord progressions • use the modes • play over
nondiatonic harmony • use harmonic and melodic minor
scales • use symmetrical scales such as chromatic, whole-
tone and diminished scales • incorporate exotic scales such
as Hungarian major and Gypsy minor • and much more!
00695563 Book/CD Pack..$14.95

SPEED MECHANICS FOR LEAD GUITAR
INCLUDES TAB

Take your playing to the stratosphere
with the most advanced lead book
by this proven heavy metal author.
Speed Mechanics is the ultimate
technique book for developing the
kind of speed and precision in
today's explosive playing styles.
Learn the fastest ways to achieve
speed and control, secrets to make your practice time really
count, and how to open your ears and make your musical
ideas more solid and tangible. Packed with over 200 vicious
exercises including Troy's scorching version of "Flight of the
Bumblebee." Music and examples demonstrated on CD.
89-minute audio.
00699323 Book/CD Pack..$19.95

TOTAL ROCK GUITAR
INCLUDES TAB

A COMPLETE GUIDE TO
LEARNING ROCK GUITAR
by Troy Stetina
This unique and comprehensive
source for learning rock guitar is
designed to develop both lead and
rhythm playing. It covers: getting a
tone that rocks • open chords,
power chords and barre chords • riffs, scales and licks •
string bending, strumming, palm muting, harmonics and
alternate picking • all rock styles • and much more. The
examples are in standard notation with chord grids and tab,
and the CD includes full-band backing for all 22 songs.
00695246 Book/CD Pack..$19.99

FOR MORE INFORMATION, SEE YOUR LOCAL MUSIC DEALER,
OR WRITE TO:

HAL•LEONARD®
CORPORATION
7777 W. BLUEMOUND RD. P.O. BOX 13819 MILWAUKEE, WI 53213

Visit Hal Leonard Online at
www.halleonard.com

Prices, contents, and availability subject to change without notice.

0809